Understanding Hamlet

A Study Guide

Understanding Hamlet

A STUDY GUIDE

ROBERT RENWICK

Holland River Press
Holland Landing, Ontario

Editors: Carina Samuels, Ashley Glovasky, Hufsa Tahir

Cover Design: Alex Damianidis

Interior Design: Hufsa Tahir

References cited in the text of *Understanding Hamlet* are drawn from *The New Clarendon Shakespeare* version of *Hamlet* (1947), edited by George Rylands, the Oxford University Press, 1978 edition.

ISBN 978-0-9947580-0-2

Version 1.0. Printed by Lightning Source. Published in Canada by Holland River Press.

TABLE OF CONTENTS

SUGGESTIONS FOR USING THIS BOOK   I

PROLOGUE   III

INTRODUCTION TO HAMLET   1

    MAIN CHARACTERS   1

    SETTING   1

    SOURCES   2

    HAMLET AS TRAGEDY   2

    BRIEF SUMMARY AND ANALYSIS OF HAMLET   3

    SYNOPSIS AND COMMENTARY   6

INTRODUCTION TO THE ESSAYS   47

A FETCH OF WARRANT   50

MIGHTY OPPOSITES   58

    I. HAMLET AND CLAUDIUS   59

    II. HAMLET AND OTHER CHARACTERS   65

    III. HAMLET'S SOLILOQUIES   75

    SUMMATION: HAMLET   79

    IV. CLAUDIUS AND OTHER CHARACTERS   80

    V. CLAUDIUS'S SOLILOQUIES   88

    SUMMATION: CLAUDIUS   90

    CONCLUSIONS   90

DEFYING AUGURY   92

FRAILTY, IS WOMAN THY TRUE NAME?   103

TO THE READER   113

ABOUT THE AUTHOR   115

For Meredith, Justin, and Lindsay Renwick

Suggestions for Using This Book

Secondary School Students

Understanding Hamlet is intended for use in conjunction with approaches your teacher takes as you work through the play in and outside of class.

The INTRODUCTION TO HAMLET section provides basic information about the play and includes an overall summary of events.

The SYNOPSIS AND COMMENTARY section contains detailed summaries of what happens scene by scene with observations and interpretations where necessary. They establish a framework for deepening the understanding of each scene as it is worked through in class or on your own, This section can be useful in reviewing for tests and examinations and in doing writing assignments and other activities.

The ESSAY section features four essays dealing with important themes in *Hamlet*. There are full descriptions of the origin of the ideas for the essays and of how each essay is organized and structured. They can serve as models to assist with the development and refining of your own writing skills. Careful study of the essays should increase understanding and appreciation of the play.

College and University Students

Post-secondary students may also profit from reading the material above. The SYNPOSIS AND COMMENTARY section can serve to refresh knowledge of events and situations in the play and act as a stimulus in thinking about them. The essays are intended to serve as examples of how, after intensive study of a literary work, particular aspects catch our attention and invite systematic investigation in written form.

Teachers

Teachers may want to use *Understanding Hamlet* as an adjunct to other approaches employed as they teach the play. The SYNOPSIS AND COMMENTARY section might be used as a source of teaching points for each scene. The comments and interpretations might act as springboards for class discussion or student writing.

Other Readers

This guide should help theatregoers and general readers deepen their understanding and appreciation of the play.

Prologue

Whenever a new study guide is published, prospective readers are bound to ask, "Aren't there enough of these already?" The question is legitimate. One short answer would be that it never hurts to take another fresh look at a masterwork. Once in a while, new insights can emerge. I hope this is the case from time to time for *Understanding Hamlet*.

A longer answer to the question is that other guides, in addition to providing detailed scene by scene summaries and relevant commentary, also contain a wealth of information not directly related to *Hamlet*. For example, brief biographies of Shakespeare, short histories of Renaissance England, accounts of the development of the Elizabethan theatre, and references to other dramatists of Shakespeare's time, as interesting as they may be, do little to deepen understanding of *Hamlet*, the play. This guide is intended to enhance understanding by focusing in detail on what happens scene by scene, and by providing original essays on significant themes meant to increase understanding and serve as models for essay writing.

Understanding Hamlet should prove useful to students, teachers, theatregoers, and general readers. I have tried to make it as accurate, straightforward, and simply expressed as possible. My hope is that on the one hand, the guide helps the play speak for itself, and that on the other, it provides a useful description and illustration of a method for reflecting formally on its meaning.

Robert Renwick
Holland Landing, Ontario
May 2015

part one

abstracts and brief chronicles

Introduction to Hamlet

Main Characters

Hamlet, Prince of Denmark: obliged to avenge the murder of his father, Old Hamlet, former King of Denmark

Claudius, King of Denmark: Hamlet's uncle, and brother to Old Hamlet; seducer of Queen Gertrude and murderer of his brother

Gertrude, Queen of Denmark: Hamlet's mother; wife to Old Hamlet, then Claudius

Polonius, Secretary of State in Denmark: close advisor to Claudius

Ophelia, daughter of Polonius: involved in an abortive love relationship with Hamlet

Laertes, son of Polonius: seeks revenge against Hamlet over the death of Polonius

Horatio: friend and confidant of Hamlet

Rosencrantz and Guildenstern, former friends of Hamlet: now in the service of Claudius and Gertrude

Fortinbras, Prince of Norway: eventual King of Denmark

Setting

The play takes place in Denmark some time during the eighth and tenth centuries AD. During this period, Denmark was a powerful nation in northwestern Europe, forming part of the Viking confederacy that had overrun and conquered parts of England and the continent during the previous two or three centuries.

Sources

As was often his practice, Shakespeare drew upon available historical sources in order to find much of the material he needed to write *Hamlet*. The earliest known version of the Hamlet story appears in Historia Danica, written by Danish historian Saxo Grammaticus in the 12th century. A French version is included in Histoires tragiques by François Belleforest, published in Paris in 1576. There was as well at least one lost version of the tragedy of *Hamlet* by another Elizabethan dramatist (probably Thomas Kyd) that predates Shakespeare's play. As he wrote and revised his version of the Hamlet story, which he began as early as 1600, Shakespeare reworked and embellished these sources to suit his purposes.

Hamlet as Tragedy

Broadly speaking, tragedies are plays in which the fortunes of a central character, called the hero, someone neither wholly good nor bad, go from happiness to misery because of a serious flaw in character or error of judgment. The immediate effects on the audience are said to be pity, because the consequences are more severe than the hero deserves, and fear, because we recognize that our own personal failings could bring misfortunes upon us. Paradoxically, however, feelings of grief and even elation tend to arise as audiences leave the theatre, perhaps because the play has served as a warning to be more aware of consequences of our own actions.

In Shakespeare's day, tragedies of revenge were performed regularly on London stages. *Hamlet* is considered the prime example of this genre. In tragedies of revenge, the central character must avenge the murder of a close relative, usually a son or father. In the process, this character has to overcome a number of challenging obstacles. By the final act, he manages to kill the villain, condemning his soul to burn forever in hellfire. Frequently, other characters, often including the central character himself, also die. Tragedies of revenge typically involve a ghost, insanity, suicide, a play-with-a-play, sensational incidents, and bloody endings.

Brief Summary and Analysis of Hamlet

In Shakespeare's play, Hamlet, is an intelligent, sensitive, introspective, somewhat unstable young man. He has recently come home from studying abroad to attend the funeral of his father, Old Hamlet, who had been King of Denmark. Hamlet was strongly attached to his father, whose death occurred suddenly and under mysterious circumstances.

Greatly aggrieved over his father's death, Hamlet resents the fact that Old Hamlet's brother, Claudius, has become king. In Hamlet's eyes, Claudius is the much lesser man. Moreover, as he admits to his friend Horatio near the play's end, Hamlet had expected that he himself would succeed his father. To make matters worse, Hamlet's mother, Queen Gertrude, married Claudius a very short time after the funeral of Old Hamlet.

As the play opens, Hamlet is moody and withdrawn. His emotional difficulties increase when the ghost of his father appears, telling Hamlet that he did not die of natural causes but was poisoned by Claudius. The ghost demands vengeance, but forbids Hamlet from punishing Gertrude. It informs the prince that Claudius seduced Gertrude before the murder took place.

Shocked at the ghost's revelations, Hamlet at first appears highly motivated to seek revenge. However, he is rather slow in going about it. In part, the delay is due to flaws in his own character, but it is also true that significant obstacles lay in his path.

Claudius is the king, a person to whom all subjects owe loyalty. Their first obligation would be to preserve his life, not end it. Moreover, Claudius is Hamlet's uncle and stepfather, a blood relative. He is also apparently very dear to Gertrude. Finally, there is a lack of hard evidence against the king. All Hamlet has to go on is the word of a ghost. In Shakespeare's day, ghosts were considered evil. Hamlet doesn't know how far to trust the ghost's word.

Because no one else hears the ghost's story, the pressure to seek revenge falls solely on Hamlet. The remainder of the play is taken up with how, in a very roundabout way and at great cost to himself and others, Hamlet succeeds in avenging his father's death.

After his meeting with the ghost, Hamlet decides to act from time to time as if he were insane. Gertrude and Claudius are greatly concerned over Hamlet's apparent lunacy, which Polonius believes is due to the termination of the prince's love relationship with his daughter, Ophelia. Polonius offers to test his theory by arranging an interview between Ophelia and Hamlet, which he and the king will observe secretly. The result proves inconclusive, but Claudius is convinced that Hamlet is sane enough and a source of potential danger. He considers sending him on a state visit to England.

Meanwhile, Claudius and Gertrude have summoned to court two old friends of Hamlet, Rosencrantz and Guildenstern, hoping they will be able to help discover the source of the prince's disturbed behavior. Suspicious of their motives, Hamlet at first greets his friends cordially, but keeps them very much at arm's length when they inquire about his affliction.

Attempting to cheer the prince up, Rosencrantz tells him of the imminent arrival of a company of travelling actors. Hamlet decides to have them perform before the entire court a play into which he introduces details of the ghost's account of the murder of Old Hamlet. When Claudius appears to act in a guilty manner during the performance, Hamlet believes he can proceed with his revenge. However, the king now knows what Hamlet suspects, and decides to send him immediately on the diplomatic mission to England. Claudius instructs Rosencrantz and Guildenstern to accompany the prince.

Earlier on, Polonius had arranged with Claudius to test his theory of the cause of Hamlet's madness one more time. Hidden behind a curtain in the queen's apartment, Polonius listens as Gertrude begins to berate her son for staging the play. When Hamlet starts to attack her verbally, the queen cries out for help. From behind the curtain, Polonius calls for help as well. Believing that it is Claudius, Hamlet stabs the old man through the curtain with his sword.

Turning on his astonished mother, the prince rebukes her for her adultery with and subsequent marriage to Claudius. Hamlet's tirade is interrupted by the reappearance of the ghost, who reproves him for his tardiness in seeking revenge against Claudius. The queen neither sees nor hears the ghost and believes her son is hallucinating. Hamlet tells her that he is not insane and makes her swear not to reveal that fact to Claudius. Thoroughly chastened, Gertrude has been won over to her son's side. Bidding his mother goodnight, Hamlet drags the corpse of Polonius out of the bedchamber.

Gertrude reports Polonius's death to Claudius, who confronts Hamlet, ordering his immediate departure for England. In an aside, Claudius reveals that he will instruct the English king to have his nephew put to death as soon as he arrives. On his way to the ship, Hamlet encounters an army led by Young Fortinbras, Prince of Norway, that is passing through Denmark on its way to fight against Poland.

News of Polonius' death brings on genuine madness in Ophelia. Her eventual death by drowning is an apparent suicide. Laertes returns from France and confronts Claudius, who he believes was responsible for his father's death. Claudius assures him that Hamlet killed Polonius. Laertes vows revenge. This desire intensifies when he learns of Ophelia's death.

Hamlet manages to abort the voyage to England by escaping onto an attacking pirate ship, which brings him back to Denmark. He tells Horatio that aboard ship he secretly discovered a warrant for his death. He says he replaced it with one ordering the deaths of Rosencrantz and Guildenstern.

Claudius and Laertes learn of Hamlet's return and plot to have the prince die in a fencing match arranged for sport with Laertes. The plot misfires. Gertrude, Laertes, Claudius, and Hamlet all die. As Horatio prepares to make Hamlet's story public, Young Fortinbras arrives from the campaign against Poland in time to take over the throne of Denmark.

Synopsis and Commentary

ACT ONE

Act I, Scene 1 SENTRIES ON NIGHTWATCH

1. A Ghost Walks the Night

On a very cold night, Francisco, a soldier in the Danish army, has been standing watch over the royal palace. At midnight, he is relieved by Bernardo and Marcellus, two officers who are accompanied by Horatio, a friend and fellow student of Prince Hamlet.

The guards seem somewhat tense as they await the possible appearance of the ghost of Old Hamlet, former king of Denmark, who has recently died under strange circumstances. Marcellus says that he and Bernardo have seen the ghost on two previous occasions. He indicates that despite Horatio's belief that their imaginations have been playing tricks, he has invited Horatio to watch with them and perhaps speak with the ghost.

Horatio scoffs at the likelihood of seeing the ghost. But as Bernardo begins an account of the circumstances of its latest appearance, the ghost of the old king, fully armed, approaches. Overcome with fear and wonder, Horatio invites the ghost to speak, but it disappears without responding. A little shamefaced, Horatio tells Bernardo and Marcellus that the visits of the ghost mean trouble for the kingdom of Denmark.

2. Denmark Prepares for War

The talk now turns to frantic preparations for war that are keeping workers in Denmark on the job night and day. Horatio tells the others that he believes the workers are making weaponry to be used to repel an anticipated invasion from Norway. According to Horatio, an army under the command of Young Fortinbras, Prince of Norway, is about to try to reclaim territory lost to the Danes many years before. The loss occurred when Old Fortinbras, then king of Norway, was slain in single combat by Old Hamlet.

As Bernardo and Horatio speculate that the appearances of the ghost bear directly on the imminent war, it returns once more.

3. The Ghost Reappears

Horatio confronts the ghost, encouraging it to speak. Before it can, the ghost suddenly withdraws. Apparently the crowing of a rooster, heralding the approach of dawn, has caused it to retreat to the world of spirits. Horatio and Marcellus agree to report what they have seen to Hamlet, anticipating that if he were to confront the ghost, it would likely speak with him.

Act I, Scene 2 IN THE COURT OF THE KING OF DENMARK

1. Claudius Addresses His Courtiers

In what is almost certainly his first council meeting as king, Claudius begins tactfully by thanking the members of court for their patience and understanding. These remarks are in regard to the foreshortened period of mourning that followed the untimely death of Old Hamlet, and to what may have appeared to be a very hasty marriage with his widow.

The king turns to the threat from Norway. Claudius repeats what we have already learned from Horatio: Fortinbras is out to regain lands lost to the Danes following the death of Old Fortinbras at the hands of Old Hamlet. Claudius adds that Young Fortinbras is evidently trying to exploit possible political weakness and instability in Denmark following the death of the old king. Furthermore, in organizing the proposed invasion, Fortinbras has been acting independent of the current king of Norway, his elderly and ailing uncle.

Claudius mentions having prepared a letter for the Norwegian king, informing him of Fortinbras's intentions and asking that he take measures to keep his nephew in check. Two of Claudius's courtiers, Cornelius and Voltimand, are to deliver the letter as speedily as possible.

2. Claudius and the Family of Polonius

Turning to Laertes, son of Polonius, his secretary of state, Claudius graciously grants Laertes' request to be allowed to return to France, where he had been living for some time. Before giving his approval, however, Claudius makes sure that Polonius has no objections.

3. Claudius and Gertrude Appeal to Hamlet

Claudius and Gertrude speak at length with Hamlet, urging him to end what they regard as his excessively long period of mourning for his father. Hamlet is abrupt in his responses to the king and queen, both of whom attempt to convince him that it is inappropriate and even unmanly to prolong one's grief over an event—the death of a father—that is an inevitable part of life. Claudius even suggests that Hamlet learn to think of him as a father, since the love he bears Hamlet is equal to that of the most loving of natural fathers.

In contrast to his decision regarding Laertes, Claudius does not look favourably on Hamlet's intention to return to university in Wittenberg. The king and Gertrude express a strong preference that he remain in Elsinore as the preeminent member of court. In an apparent rebuff of Claudius, Hamlet says he will comply with his mother's wishes in this matter.

Claudius expresses joy and satisfaction at Hamlet's words. As he and Gertrude prepare to quit the council chamber, Claudius promises to celebrate Hamlet's decision at a drinking party later in the day.

4. Hamlet's First Soliloquy

Alone and melancholy, Hamlet says his dissatisfaction with the present state of the world makes him yearn for death. He identifies the sources of his despair—the death of his father, whom he regarded as infinitely superior to Claudius, and his mother's decision to wed such an unsuitable husband so quickly. Declaring the marriage "incestuous," Hamlet predicts that it is bound to be quite troubled. He is heartbroken over having to keep these disquieting thoughts to himself.

5. Hamlet Hears About the Ghost

Accompanied by Marcellus and Bernardo, Horatio greets Hamlet as though for the first time. This passage is somewhat puzzling, given that Horatio left Wittenberg for Elsinore to attend the funeral of Old Hamlet and stayed on for the wedding of Claudius and Gertrude.

After a bitter remark from Hamlet regarding the wedding, Horatio describes the encounter with the ghost. Hamlet becomes animated, launching into a series of questions intended to determine if the ghost was truly Old Hamlet's. Satisfied, Hamlet tells his companions he will join them on the platform that night. He says he will speak with the ghost if it appears.

Hamlet cautions the men to keep strict silence about the ghost. After they have left, he remarks that the ghost's visits suggest that his father's death was not accidental.

Act I, Scene 3 IN THE HOUSEHOLD OF POLONIUS

1. Laertes Takes Leave of Ophelia

About to depart for France, Laertes gets Ophelia to promise to stay in touch with him. He warns Ophelia that the love Hamlet has professed for her is not deep and not likely to last. Laertes allows that because Hamlet is just approaching manhood, his protestations are probably sincere enough. He argues, however, that as Hamlet matures, he will assume more and more his role of prince of Denmark and eventually become king. Therefore the choice of a mate will not be his.

Laertes tells his sister it would be most unwise to allow Hamlet to have his way with her. He adds that youth is a time of hot blood and high passion, when it is easy to lose control over oneself. Agreeing to heed Laertes' warning, Ophelia urges him in matters of the heart to be sure to follow his own advice.

2. Polonius Counsels His Children

Polonius appears, giving Laertes lengthy instructions on how to conduct his affairs when he is abroad. They involve prudence, moderation, and good taste. He ends by advising his son always to be true to himself.

When Laertes is gone, Polonius turns to Ophelia, chiding her for having spent so much time in the company of Hamlet. He demands that she reveal exactly what she and the prince have been up to. When Ophelia says that Hamlet has on several occasions declared his honourable love for her, Polonius calls the declarations false and insists that Hamlet's intentions are not honourable. He tells Ophelia not to see him so frequently and not to take his words of love seriously. Finally, he orders her to stop seeing Hamlet altogether. Somewhat reluctantly, she promises to obey.

Act I, Scene 4 HAMLET AND THE GHOST PART I

1. Hamlet and Horatio Discuss the Danish Reputation for Reveling

Waiting on the platform for the ghost to appear, Hamlet and Horatio hear noises from the drinking party Claudius is hosting. When Horatio asks if such activity is customary in Denmark, Hamlet acknowledges that it is, and that because he was born a Dane, he too has been affected by it. However, he says that to his mind, his countrymen would be better advised to moderate their drinking, since it tarnishes their reputation among other nations, detracting from the many accomplishments of the Danish people. As an analogy, he mentions how in an otherwise outstanding person there may be one glaring fault that ruins what would have been an unblemished reputation.

2. The Ghost Appears

Suddenly the ghost of Old Hamlet materializes. In an agitated state Hamlet confronts and challenges it. He asks whether the ghost's intentions are for good or ill, then demands to know why it has come back from the grave and what it wishes of him.

The ghost beckons Hamlet away from Horatio and Marcellus. As he begins to follow after it, his friends attempt to restrain him, arguing that the ghost could be leading him into great danger. Threatening them bodily, Hamlet tears himself away and runs after the ghost. Still concerned for his safety, Horatio and Marcellus decide to follow him.

Act I, Scene 5 HAMLET AND THE GHOST PART II

1. The Story of the Murder

When they are alone, the ghost tells Hamlet that because of serious misdeeds committed when he was alive, he is condemned for a time to walk the earth during the night and burn in purgatory in the daytime.

The ghost stuns Hamlet by revealing that Old Hamlet's death was not caused by a snakebite, which was the official explanation. Instead, having seduced and won the affections of Queen Gertrude, Claudius poured a highly poisonous substance (henbane) into Old Hamlet's ear canal while he was asleep in his orchard. The ghost complains of having died with his sins unforgiven, with no opportunity for shriving.

2. The Ghost's Exhortation

As dawn is about to force him back to his "prison house," the ghost urges Hamlet to avenge the murder. However, it forbids him to take any action against Gertrude for her infidelity. She is to be left to answer to God for her sins and suffer in life sharp pangs of remorse.

3. Hamlet's Second Soliloquy

When the ghost leaves, Hamlet becomes manic. He promises repeatedly to remember what the ghost has said, and condemns Claudius for his treachery and Gertrude for her wickedness.

4. Horatio and Marcellus Rejoin Hamlet

When Horatio and Marcellus catch up with Hamlet, he utters "wild and whirling words," the gist of which is that he will reveal nothing the ghost has told him. Hamlet does say that he believes the ghost spoke true. He swears the men to secrecy regarding what they have seen that night. The voice of the ghost urges them to take the oath.

Telling Horatio and Marcellus he will begin to act from time to time in an apparently deranged manner, Hamlet asks them to swear never to reveal that this "antic disposition" is not genuine. Prompted again by the ghost, they comply.

Hamlet promises to continue being a loving friend to Horatio and Marcellus. As they are about to part, he speaks unhappily about the disorder rampant in the kingdom and the burden he must assume in dealing with it.

ACT TWO

Act II, Scene 1 POLONIUS AND HIS CHILDREN

1. Polonius Sends a Servant on a Spy Mission

Polonius is about to send his servant Reynaldo to spy on Laertes, who is back in France. Polonius tells him to use an indirect approach in carrying out his mission. Reynaldo is to seek out other Danes in Paris who know Laertes. In conversation he is to let on that he barely knows Laertes but believes him to be somewhat immoral. Reynaldo is to note their responses and report back.

When Reynaldo questions this approach, Polonius explains that the indirect method often yields more detailed information than direct inquiry would. As Reynaldo is about to leave, Polonius tells him also to observe Laertes at first hand. Then he instructs him to allow Laertes latitude to do as he wishes, presumably to gain a truer picture of how he conducts himself.

2. Ophelia Tells Her Father a Strange Tale

Very distraught, Ophelia runs to her father, reporting that a half-dressed Hamlet had burst into her room, pale and apparently lovesick. She says he seized her roughly by the arm, staring at her for many minutes. Then with a prolonged and powerful sigh, he released her, continuing to stare as he backed out of the room.

Apparently Hamlet is making good here on his intention to act as if he were deranged. He may also be angry with Ophelia for breaking off their relationship. His behaviour is achieving a double purpose, punishing her and creating a convincing impression that he is in fact insane.

Polonius concludes that Hamlet's love for Ophelia must be genuine and that the terminating of their relationship is causing Hamlet's disturbed behaviour. The old man berates himself for believing that Hamlet was merely trifling with Ophelia.

Polonius decides to report the matter to the king. He believes that suppressing it could create more difficulty than disclosing would. He apparently suspects that Claudius may not be pleased to learn of Hamlet's affection for Ophelia.

Act II, Scene 2 VARIOUS GOINGS-ON IN THE ROYAL PALACE

1. Claudius and Gertrude Recruit Rosencrantz and Guildenstern

Claudius welcomes Hamlet's longtime friends Rosencrantz and Guildenstern to court. He asks them for help in understanding the cause of Hamlet's madness. Gertrude speaks of the close relationship they have had with Hamlet and promises them a handsome reward if they are successful. Happy to cooperate, Rosencrantz and Guildenstern leave in search of the prince.

2. Two Pieces of News for the King

Polonius approaches Claudius, indicating that Cornelius and Voltimand have returned successfully from Norway. He announces that he believes he has found the cause of Hamlet's madness, which he proposes to reveal once the ambassadors have made their report.

While Polonius leaves to usher them in, Gertrude tells Claudius that despite whatever Polonius may say, she believes Old Hamlet's death and their "o'erhasty marriage" are responsible for the prince's madness.

(a) The Ambassadors' Report

Voltimand tells Claudius that Old Norway was deceived into believing that the army raised by Young Fortinbras was planning an invasion of Poland. He has therefore reprimanded his nephew and made him vow never again to take up arms against Denmark. Fortinbras's army will undertake instead an expedition against Poland. Old Norway is requesting that Claudius grant this army safe conduct through Denmark. Claudius consents, indicating that he'll attend to the details later.

(b) Polonius Puts His Case

In his roundabout manner, Polonius assures Claudius and Gertrude that he has discovered with absolute certainty the cause of Hamlet's madness. He reads aloud from a love letter Hamlet had recently sent to Ophelia. The letter sounds sincere both in content and tone. In poetry and prose Hamlet assures her that his love is absolute and beyond doubt. Polonius adds that Ophelia has revealed that on other occasions and in various ways, Hamlet has declared his love.

When Claudius asks about Ophelia's responses, Polonius replies that as the king's true and honest servant, he made clear to her that Hamlet's station in life far exceeded hers. Therefore he instructed Ophelia to keep herself from Hamlet and receive no further love tokens. He assures the king and queen that Hamlet's insanity is simply the result of being denied access to Ophelia.

When Claudius asks for the queen's opinion, she replies that the theory might well be true. Perhaps Gertrude has been persuaded, but it might also be that this theory helps reduce guilt feelings she may have over betraying Old Hamlet and marrying Claudius. Despite Polonius's assurances, Claudius remains unconvinced. In order to test the theory, Polonius proposes to arrange a meeting between Ophelia and Hamlet that he and Claudius will overhear from behind a tapestry. The king approves the plan.

3. Polonius Engages Hamlet in Brief Conversation

This is the first time we see Hamlet affecting the "antic disposition." Absorbed in a book, Hamlet encounters Polonius, who asks if the prince recognizes him. Hamlet calls him a "fishmonger" (Elizabethan slang for the father of a prostitute) and makes lewd remarks concerning Ophelia.

When Polonius inquires about the book Hamlet has been reading, the prince pretends to quote disparaging remarks about old men. Many apply specifically to Polonius, who fails to understand that the prince is mocking him. Ironically, Polonius says that Hamlet's utterances contain as much sense as nonsense. He is too obtuse to realize that the prince is having him on.

After Polonius leaves, Hamlet's words "These tedious old fools!" indicate he has had his wits about him. He has been using his apparent madness as an excuse for demeaning Polonius.

4. Hamlet Reunited With Rosencrantz and Guildenstern

Hamlet welcomes Rosencrantz and Guildenstern warmly to Elsinore. They respond with equal warmth. The three jest briefly about the private parts of Dame Fortune.

Hamlet observes bitterly that he considers Denmark one of the worst prisons in the world. Rosencrantz takes exception, suggesting that thwarted ambition causes him to think in this manner. Perhaps Rosencrantz believes that Hamlet expected to succeed his father as king.

The three men engage in some brief intellectual sparring about relations among ambitions, shadows, and dreams. Hamlet appears to prevail.

Catching his two friends off guard, Hamlet accuses them of being summoned to Elsinore by the king and queen. Although they at first deny it, Hamlet shames them into admitting that in fact they were "sent for." Here the prince demonstrates that he is both shrewd and perceptive.

Hamlet tells his friends he is forewarned and most unlikely to reveal anything worth reporting to the king. He remarks at considerable length that his life has lately grown quite drab and joyless. Rosencrantz says this is most unfortunate, since a group of travelling actors is about to arrive in Elsinore. He fears Hamlet will be unable to receive them with his customary cheer.

The prince's mood brightens. He and Rosencrantz and Guildenstern enter into a lengthy discussion of the recent trend in Shakespeare's day of using young boys to displace older actors on London stages. This matter would have caught the attention of Elizabethan audiences but does little to advance the plot of *Hamlet*. It does compare the displacing of capable veteran actors by less talented boys to Claudius's succeeding his much worthier brother on the throne of Denmark. This remark seems ill-advised, since it may reach the king's ear.

With the players about to arrive, Hamlet welcomes his friends again, observing somewhat cryptically that Claudius and Gertrude are deceived about his apparent madness. He tells them he is "but mad north-north-west." Again this observation could soon get back to the king and queen.

5. Hamlet Welcomes the Travelling Players

Polonius announces the arrival of the players. Affecting his "antic disposition," Hamlet mocks the old man once more, likening him to Jephthah, a biblical figure who had inadvertently placed the life of his daughter in jeopardy.

In high spirits, Hamlet welcomes the actors, asking the First Player to recite part of a favourite speech. The prince cues him by speaking the first few lines. The speech comes from a play dealing with the fall of the ancient city of Troy. Aeneas is speaking to Dido, Queen of Carthage, long after escaping the burning city. The subject is the death of King Priam of Troy. Priam was slain by Pyrrhus, son of Achilleus, who had been killed by Priam's son Paris.

This passage may appeal to Hamlet largely because its theme is a son's obligation to avenge his father's death. It mentions the momentary inability of Pyrrhus to take revenge upon Priam, a situation which parallels Hamlet's own delay in acting against Claudius. The speech ends with a reference to the grief-stricken Hecuba, wife of Priam, at which point tears well up in the eyes of the First Player.

Hamlet stops the recitation, directing Polonius to ensure the players are properly lodged in the castle. Drawing the First Player aside, he asks the company to perform a tragedy, *The Murder of Gonzago*, on the next evening. Hamlet arranges with the First Player to incorporate into it lines that he himself will write.

6. Hamlet's Third Soliloquy

Alone on the stage, Hamlet berates himself at length over his failure to avenge his father's death. He marvels at the First Player's ability to become emotionally aroused over the plight of Hecuba, a character from fiction, whereas he has been unable to motivate himself to avenge the murder of someone important and real. Hamlet wonders if he has failed to take action against Claudius because he lacks courage to do so.

Hamlet's train of thought switches to his need for greater certainty regarding the circumstances of his father's death. He decides to include in the upcoming performance a number of the details the ghost had mentioned. Hamlet concludes that if while witnessing the play, Claudius reacts in an incriminating manner, he will have the evidence he needs. He'll also know that the ghost was not leading him to his doom.

The decision to stage this play is an interesting turn of events. It's true that the ghost's story is unsubstantiated. It's possible that the staging of *The Murder of Gonzago*, somewhat amended, could either confirm or call into question in Hamlet's mind the accuracy of the ghost's story. However, a failure on the part of Claudius to react suspiciously would not necessarily contradict it. The king might be skilled at dissembling or completely lacking in conscience. We learn in his soliloquies that Claudius is troubled over what he has done, but Hamlet is unaware of that fact.

Moreover, an incriminating reaction from Claudius that falls short of an outright confession would not constitute hard evidence of his guilt. In order to justify taking revenge, Hamlet would need hard evidence. The decision to stage the play involves considerable personal risk to Hamlet. After seeing it, Claudius would know with absolute certainty that Hamlet is on to him. The king would have little choice. He'd need to act swiftly against his nephew. All things considered, it's difficult to see how much Hamlet really stands to gain from having the players reenact the murder.

ACT THREE

Act III, Scene 1 HAMLET'S MADNESS UNDER SCRUTINY

1. Rosencrantz and Guildenstern Report to the King and Queen
Claudius expresses impatience with the inability of Rosencrantz and Guildenstern to discover the source of Hamlet's lunacy. They inform the king that the prince has been much less than cooperative with them.

When Gertrude asks if they have managed to involve Hamlet in pleasurable pursuits, Rosencrantz and Guildenstern mention the arrival of the travelling players and Hamlet's decision to have them perform that night.

As Hamlet had requested, Polonius invites the king and queen to attend the performance. Ironically, Claudius is pleased at this development, little realizing that he is walking into a clever trap. He even tells Rosencrantz and Guildenstern to encourage Hamlet in this endeavour.

2. Preparations For Testing Polonius's Theory

Claudius shares with Gertrude the details of the spying activity he and Polonius are up to. The queen hopes that it will reveal that Hamlet's madness really is due to thwarted love for Ophelia. She remarks that restoration of that relationship should make him whole again.

Polonius attends to final arrangements for the spying. Instructing Ophelia to pretend to be reading from a holy book, he reproaches himself for glossing over shameful behaviour by associating it with religion.

This remark produces a pang of conscience in Claudius, which he speaks of in an aside. This is the first indication that the king is capable of remorse. It also lends credence to the words of the ghost.

3. Hamlet's Fourth Soliloquy

In a despondent mood, Hamlet considers taking his own life in order to escape his difficulties. He reasons, however, that because the afterlife might well be fraught with perils considerably worse than those left behind, most people prefer to struggle on. This appears to be the course of action he will take. Hamlet observes that too much thinking about "enterprises of great pitch and moment" can undermine the motivation necessary to carry them out. No doubt he has in mind his need to avenge his father's death.

The prince reveals a limited degree of self-understanding here. He has just talked himself out of taking his own life on grounds that may appear logical. It is certain that there is no return from the afterlife. By no means does it follow, however, that the afterlife will present more daunting challenges than we face in this life. Yet he appears to use this sort of uncertainty to give himself license not to act against the king.

Hamlet hesitates to take his own life or Claudius's because results of possible actions are hard to predict. He may be asking himself implicitly if killing of Claudius would in some way make matters worse for himself than continuing to delay. What he keeps saying, however, is that excessive thinking about killing the king keeps getting in his way. But what ought to be clear is that no matter how long and hard one thinks about outcomes, it is only by taking action that results occur. To this point, Hamlet appears to prefer thinking to acting. But he blames his long hesitation on his tendency to think too much when it's really his reluctance to act that's in question.

4. Hamlet Gives Ophelia Short Shrift (The Nunnery Scene)

With Polonius and Claudius hidden behind an arras, Ophelia approaches Hamlet. Throughout their conversation, he treats her in a harsh, demeaning manner. He may be angry with her for breaking off their relationship, or perhaps he no longer trusts her because her father works so closely with Claudius. Hamlet may also suspect that this meeting is being monitored.

Ophelia begins by returning love tokens or letters she no longer wishes to keep because the giver has proved "unkind." There's a curious note of ambivalence here. When ordered to do so, Ophelia agreed rather unwillingly to break off her relationship with Hamlet. She now appears unhappy with his treatment of her, perhaps as a result of Hamlet's unsettling visit to her sewing room.

Hamlet rails against women in general and Ophelia in partic-ular, deploring the fact that beautiful women are rarely able to remain chaste. He admits that he once did love her, then immediately denies it. He admits to numerous faults himself, declaring the vast majority of men "arrant knaves." He advises Ophelia to enter a nunnery, which is also Elizabethan slang for a brothel. Hamlet may intend that both meanings apply.

Perhaps sensing they are not alone, the prince suddenly asks where Polonius is. When Ophelia says he's at home, Hamlet calls him a fool who ought to be locked up there.

The prince continues his tirade against women, advising Ophelia never to marry. Should she disregard this advice, he tells her to wed a fool, since wise men well know that wives are likely to be unfaithful. Deploring the vain and lecherous nature of women, Hamlet calls for the abolition of marriage. Then he makes a cryptic remark about one married person (likely Claudius) who will not continue to live. Hamlet tells Ophelia again to enter a nunnery. When he is gone, she expresses shock and great distress over Hamlet's mental state. Ophelia still cares for him and truly believes he is mad.

It seems likely that Hamlet is displacing onto Ophelia much of the anger he feels toward his mother. No doubt Ophelia has hurt and offended him, but she was ordered to end their relationship. Even if Hamlet is not aware that Polonius forced her hand, his outbursts are unjustifiably harsh. If his purpose was simply to affect the "antic disposition," he has gone much too far.

5. Claudius and Polonius Disagree

Claudius dismisses the forbidden love theory and pronounces Hamlet sane enough. The king anticipates danger to himself when Hamlet stops brooding over his troubles and decides to take action. Claudius proposes to send him to England on state business, hoping a change of scenery will improve his mood.

Unwilling to abandon his theory, Polonius suggests a further testing. It would involve a meeting between Hamlet and the queen, which Polonius would observe secretly. Claudius tells him to proceed, stressing the need to keep the prince under close watch.

Act III, Scene 2 THE MOUSE-TRAP

1. Hamlet's Injunctions to the Players

Shakespeare uses Hamlet as a mouthpiece to air complaints about the excesses of rival companies of players in London in the late 16th century. He instructs the travelling players to speak their lines in a lively manner which is moderate and restrained. He orders them to avoid the ranting and posturing typical of contemporary actors.

According to Hamlet, the function of drama is to hold a mirror up to nature, showing the world as it truly is. This function, he maintains, should be performed in an understated fashion. Hamlet particularly objects to actors who strut and bellow, and to those who in low comic roles play for extra laughs and detract from the seriousness of the drama.

The First Player assures Hamlet all will be as he wishes. Polonius tells the prince that Claudius and Gertrude will witness the performance.

2. Hamlet and Horatio Plot Strategy

Drawing Horatio aside, Hamlet praises him at length for his justness, steadfastness, and stability. He says he particularly admires Horatio because he is not much affected by the "buffets and rewards" of fortune, and does not suffer from an overly emotional nature. The contrast with Hamlet's own temperament is evident.

As they prepare for the performance, we learn that Hamlet has informed Horatio of the details of the ghost's story. He asks Horatio to watch Claudius's reactions to the play closely and compare notes with him afterward. Horatio promises to be vigilant.

3. Preliminaries to the Performance

Claudius, Gertrude, and various members of court appear. Claudius greets Hamlet, whose responses are baffling and impertinent. His antic disposition is at work again.

Turning to Polonius, Hamlet makes light of the old man's career as an amateur actor. His blatantly sexual remarks to Ophelia cause her to make mild objections. Hamlet complains about how easily Gertrude has forgotten her first husband.

In a dumb-show the performers enact the principal events of the play. They include the pouring of poison into the ear of a sleeping king.

Apparently, Claudius and Gertrude are occupied with other matters and do not see it.

4. The King Rises to the Bait

When the performance begins, the Player King and Queen speak at length about how happy and satisfactory their thirty-year marriage has been. Mindful of his ill health, the Player Queen confesses that she fears for him. She assures him, however, that her love has never been stronger.

The Player King tells her he is soon to die, but expresses hope that she will be fortunate in her choice of a second husband. The Player Queen rules out the possibility of remarriage, indicating that it would amount to a betrayal. She says the only women who remarry are those who have killed their first husband. The Player Queen insists a second marriage amounts to killing the first husband again.

The Player King believes she is sincere, but says that noble intentions are often weakened with the passing of time. This comment is as applicable to Hamlet as it might be to the Player Queen.

The Player King observes that, when someone's fortune is in decline, those very close to him often drift away, attaching themselves to others. He predicts that despite her good intentions, the Player Queen will change her mind fairly quickly.

She replies that she would wish to be denied food, daylight, recreation, rest, and liberty if she ever breaks her vow. Were she to wed again, she says all her desires would be denied and she would live in everlasting torment. Impressed with her seriousness, the Player King begs leave to take a nap.

These exchanges between the Player King and Queen may be part of what Hamlet was to insert in the play. The references to remarried women having killed their first husband apply tangentially to Gertrude. The devotion shown by the Player Queen could be considered Hamlet's idealized version of the relationship that should have existed between his parents.

When Hamlet asks Gertrude for her opinion of the play, she says that the Player Queen overstates her case. The queen has a point. The Player Queen's assurances are excessive. The remark may also spring from Gertrude's bad conscience. Hamlet tells his mother that the Player Queen will be true to her word.

An apprehensive Claudius asks Hamlet if the play contains any offensive material. Hamlet admits that some bad business is about to occur. However, he assures Claudius that neither of them should be affected by it, since they each have a clear conscience.

Turning to Ophelia, Hamlet makes more lewd remarks. Then he speaks of a murder about to be committed. The villain pours poison into the ear of the sleeping Player King.

Claudius reacts in a startled manner. Calling for torches to be lit, he withdraws immediately to his chambers.

5. Aftermath

Alone with Horatio, Hamlet utters wild-sounding words in celebration of the apparent success of his strategy. He and Horatio agree that Claudius has definitely implicated himself.

Guildenstern tells Hamlet that Claudius is extremely angry. Hamlet suggests that the king consult a physician over the excess of bile responsible for the anger. He adds that if he were to attempt to relieve the king's symptoms, Claudius would only become worse.

Guildenstern gives way to Rosencrantz, who tells the prince that Gertrude is very upset and wishes to speak with him in her bed-chamber. When Hamlet consents, Rosencrantz asks him why he carries on as he does. The prince cites frustration at having to wait to succeed Claudius as king of Denmark.

Hamlet seizes a woodwind instrument from one of the actors. Thrusting it at Guildenstern, he demands he play a tune on it. When Guildenstern says he cannot, Hamlet tells him it is as difficult to pry information out of him as it would be to play the instrument.

Polonius enters, instructing Hamlet to go directly to the queen. Hamlet mocks the old man, asking if a cloud overhead is shaped like a camel, weasel, or whale. He tells Polonius that he will come to Gertrude when he is ready to.

6. Hamlet's Fifth Soliloquy

On his way to Gertrude's chamber, Hamlet remarks that it is now the time of night when the powers of evil hold sway, an appropriate moment to undertake action too dire for the daytime.

However, his mother is on his mind now, not Claudius. Hamlet speaks of a momentary urge to take her life, as the Roman emperor Nero did with his mother. He resolves instead to "speak daggers to her."

Hamlet's apparent desire to kill Gertrude may represent a displacement of his anger away from Claudius and onto a less threatening target. Hamlet has the evidence he maintained was sufficient to justify killing the king. Instead, he focuses on Gertrude, who according to the ghost was guilty only of adultery. The ghost also forbade Hamlet to act against his mother. It's Claudius that Hamlet needs to deal with. He appears to be procrastinating again.

Act III, Scene 3 A NEAR MISS

1. Another Assignment for Rosencrantz and Guildenstern

Speaking with Rosencrantz and Guildenstern, Claudius expresses a strong dislike of Hamlet. He says he feels no longer safe with this madman on the loose.

Claudius orders them to leave immediately with Hamlet on a voyage to England. They are eager to go, speaking of the obligation all subjects have to ensure the safety of the king. Although Claudius offers no response, these remarks may have prompted in part the feelings he will express shortly in soliloquy.

Urging a quick departure, the king stresses the need to keep Hamlet on a tight rein.

2. Preparations for the Second Testing of Polonius's Theory

Polonius tells Claudius that he is on his way to hide in Gertrude's bedchamber to hear the conversation between her and Hamlet. He promises to report before the king goes to bed.

3. Claudius's Soliloquy

Alone on the stage, Claudius says that his brother's murder weighs heavy on his conscience. He considers praying for forgiveness but hesitates because his guilt gives rise to ambivalent feelings. The king seems convinced that God's mercy is sufficient to forgive a sin as grievous as fratricide, that one cannot conceive of mercy unless there are sins that need forgiveness. He maintains that prayer can serve a double function. It can prevent an evil deed from occurring or bring about absolution after such an act. Claudius decides to "look up" for forgiveness.

Quickly however, the king realizes that he can hardly expect forgiveness when he possesses all the rewards the murder has brought him. Whereas money and power can forestall the course of justice in this world, there is no such influence in the next. There one must be accountable for his sins.

Claudius considers repenting but decides he cannot. He is more troubled than ever. Struggling to free himself of guilt, he has become more enmeshed in it. Calling upon angels for help, he bends his knees in prayer.

4. Hamlet's Sixth Soliloquy

Stumbling upon Claudius, Hamlet considers killing him on the spot. He quickly stops himself, reasoning that killing the king at prayer would send his soul to heaven all sins forgiven.

He believes that slaying Claudius now would spare him all the torment the ghost of Old Hamlet endures. Hamlet decides to wait to catch the king in some grossly sinful act. He continues on to his mother's bedchamber.

Claudius rises, his attempt at prayer futile. Hamlet's rationale for postponing his revenge is undercut. He had, however, no way of knowing of Claudius's inability to pray. The prince continues on his way to meet his mother.

Act III, Scene 4 HAMLET REBUKES HIS MOTHER

1. Polonius and Gertrude

About to conceal himself, Polonius directs Gertrude to tell her son that his misbehaviour will not be tolerated. She is to remind Hamlet that she has often intervened to protect him. Gertrude promises to cooperate.

2. Hamlet and Gertrude (The Closet Scene)

(a) The Death of Polonius

Hamlet enters Gertrude's bedchamber, treating her disrespectfully. He holds a mirror up to her so she can see herself as she truly is. Afraid for her life, Gertrude cries for help. Polonius echoes her words from behind the arras.

Believing that Claudius cried out, Hamlet thrusts his rapier through the arras, killing Polonius. Gertrude blames Hamlet for this "rash and bloody deed." He says it is almost as bad as a woman killing a king and marrying his brother. Gertrude seems astonished at this remark. Her reaction suggests that she was not party to the murder of Old Hamlet.

Hamlet bids a harsh, unfeeling farewell to Polonius. He says he intends to attack his mother with words of censure and blame.

(b) Hamlet Speaks Daggers

The queen demands to know what she has done to make Hamlet speak this way. He shows her two pictures, one of Old Hamlet and one of Claudius. Hamlet likens Old Hamlet to a Roman god or a beautiful mountain, and Claudius to a rotting ear of corn or a flat, barren place.

He accuses Gertrude of being a very bad judge of men. He says the devil himself must have impaired her senses because a woman deprived of almost every one of her senses would know that Claudius does not begin to compare with Old Hamlet. He asks what hope there can be for younger people when they select lovers if older people can be as blind as Gertrude.

Hamlet's words cut her deeply. The queen begs him to stop, but the tirade continues.

(c) An Unexpected Visitor

The ghost of Old Hamlet intervenes, urging Hamlet to get on with his revenge. Unable to see or hear the ghost, Gertrude thinks Hamlet is hallucinating and expresses great concern for him. Hamlet cannot understand why his mother does not see the ghost.

He tells the ghost its pitiable manner makes his resolution to carry out the revenge weaken. After the ghost departs, Gertrude blames the hallucination on Hamlet's madness.

(d) Hamlet Confides In The Queen

Hamlet assures Gertrude that he is as sane as she. He tells her that her great sin of marrying Claudius causes him to speak so harshly. He urges her to repent and cease further sinning. Gertrude says Hamlet's words are tearing her apart.

Hamlet urges his mother to avoid Claudius's bed. He says that once she begins to distance herself from him it will get easier to do so. The prince expresses brief regret over killing Polonius. He regards it as a punishment by the gods on himself and the old man. Hamlet promises to remove the corpse and take full responsibility for the killing. He makes the queen promise not to tell Claudius that he is pretending to be insane.

(e) Hamlet's Immediate Future

Hamlet speaks of his imminent departure for England in the company of Rosencrantz and Guildenstern, whom he says he no longer trusts. He tells Gertrude that he plans to bring them to a bad end. The prince promises to drag the body of Polonius to an adjoining room. He says that the killing will hasten his departure. He remarks that the foolhardy old man is now a more discreet counsellor than he ever was in life.

ACT FOUR

Act IV, Scene 1 CLAUDIUS UNDER DURESS

Gertrude encounters Claudius, who asks why she is so agitated. She tells him that in a fit of madness Hamlet has slain Polonius.

Claudius's reaction is not of grief or amazement over the death of his trusted adviser. Instead, Claudius remarks that Hamlet could just as easily have killed him had he been behind the arras. The king says he rather than Hamlet will have to answer for this death, since he should have kept his nephew under closer watch.

When Claudius asks where Hamlet has gone, Gertrude says he is attending to the corpse and is full of regret. Gertrude is more than keeping the promises she made in the previous scene. Her words indicate that her son's madness is genuine, even though Hamlet had assured her that it isn't. The statement about Hamlet's misgivings over Polonius's death flies in the face of his "foolish prating knave" remark and others in the previous scene.

Claudius decides to send Hamlet overseas at sunrise. He tells Gertrude he will have to make excuses for what the prince has done. The king asks Rosencrantz and Guildenstern to find Hamlet and bring the corpse of Polonius to the chapel.

Claudius tells Gertrude that they'll have to let members of the court know about the death and what is being done about it. He hopes to be able to escape blame, and says he is very sick at heart.

Act IV, Scene 2 AN UNCOOPERATIVE PRINCE

Having placed Polonius's body under a staircase, Hamlet encounters Rosencrantz and Guildenstern. When they ask where he has put the body, the prince answers evasively. He mocks Rosencrantz, referring to him as a "sponge" that for the present soaks up the king's favour but will eventually be squeezed dry and cast aside. When Rosencrantz says he does not understand, the prince tells him indirectly that he is a fool. Agreeing to go to the king, Hamlet runs off as if playing a game of hide-and-seek.

Act IV, Scene 3 CLAUDIUS SENDS HAMLET PACKING

Claudius tells members of court how dangerous Hamlet has become. He says he would treat him more harshly were he not so popular with the common people. He stresses that the decision to send Hamlet to England must not appear impulsive. Nonetheless, the king insists that serious diseases require strong medicine.

Rosencrantz reports no success in finding the body. When Guildenstern and Hamlet appear, the prince treats Claudius in a roundabout and insolent manner. He suggests at one point that the king go to hell, if need be, to seek the old man. Then he reveals the body's location. Adopting a reassuring tone, Claudius tells Hamlet that a quick departure for England will ensure his safety. Appearing eager to go, Hamlet refers to Claudius mockingly as his "mother."

Claudius tells Rosencrantz and Guildenstern to get Hamlet on board ship that night. In a short soliloquy, he reveals that he is ordering the English king, one of his vassals, to see that Hamlet is executed on arrival. Claudius says he will never rest easy until Hamlet is dead.

Hamlet's willingness to undertake this voyage is difficult to understand. He must realize that it would delay his revenge for a considerable time. Hamlet still appears to lack the resolve necessary to kill Claudius.

Act IV, Scene 4 ONE PRINCE INSPIRES ANOTHER

1. The Forces of Young Fortinbras on the March

In command of a Norwegian army on its way to Poland, Young Fortinbras sends a messenger to Claudius. He is to inform the king that Fortinbras wishes to use the safe conduct granted earlier. Fortinbras says that if any discussion is necessary, he will readily comply. He marches on with the rest of his troops.

On their way to the ship, Hamlet and Rosencrantz and Guildenstern encounter the army but do not see Young Fortinbras. Hamlet learns from one of the soldiers that they are out to conquer a small almost valueless piece of land that will be staunchly defended by the Polacks.

The prince says this absurd situation is the result of a lengthy period of peace and prosperity, which has left the two armies simply spoiling for a fight. The situation is analogous he maintains to a large abscess in a human body that must discharge itself even though the effects will prove fatal.

2. Hamlet's Seventh Soliloquy

Hamlet uses the opposing armies as an inspiration to get on with avenging his father's death. He takes himself to task for his inactivity, arguing he has not used his intellect to its fullest extent in pursuing revenge. He speculates that he may have made himself oblivious to the task. He wonders if, in a cowardly manner, he has thought about it from so many perspectives that his will to carry it out has diminished. Reconsidering, Hamlet assures himself that he has just cause, adequate willpower, and sufficient strength to take revenge.

Hamlet cites the example of Young Fortinbras, about to put everything at risk for almost no reason, whereas he has ample justification for killing Claudius. Observing that the truly great normally need compelling reasons to take action, he adds that when a matter of honour is involved, even the slightest provocation should be reason enough to act.

Hamlet sees twenty thousand soldiers ready to die for a moment of glory. He declares that from now on that if his thoughts are not bloody they will be worthless. He sounds resolved to kill Claudius. But it is thoughts that he mentions, not actions.

Act IV, Scene 5 MORE PROBLEMS FOR CLAUDIUS AND GERTRUDE

Much time has passed since the previous scene. Laertes has returned from France after receiving news of his father's death. He has learned that Polonius's funeral was arranged hurriedly and without proper ceremony. In a later scene, we discover that Hamlet is back in Denmark after cutting short the mission to England.

1. Ophelia Distraught

A gentleman urges a reluctant Gertrude to grant audience to Ophelia. He says that her somewhat disjointed remarks about her father have been creating suspicion and doubt in those who hear them. Horatio urges Gertrude to agree to see Ophelia so others may not think the worse of herself and Claudius.

The queen is persuaded. In an aside, she complains of feeling sinful and guilty, and fears that matters will become worse.

When Ophelia appears, she begins to sing of a lover who went to the grave perhaps unmourned by his beloved. The song may refer indirectly to the incomplete and largely secret burial rites accorded Polonius. When Claudius greets her, Ophelia breaks into a song of seduction for which Claudius reproves her.

About to leave, Ophelia becomes more coherent, expressing sadness over Polonius's burial. She says she is certain Laertes will learn of it. Summoning an imaginary coach to take her away, she bids "sweet ladies" good night. The king sends others after her.

2. Claudius Unburdens Himself

Alone with the queen, Claudius expresses concern over Ophelia's breakdown. He speaks of all their recent troubles: Polonius's death;

Hamlet's removal to England; the uneasy reaction among the Danish people to the death of Polonius; the ill-advised decision to bury him quickly; Ophelia's mental state; the secret return of Laertes, who has apparently been informed by idle tongues that Claudius was responsible for Polonius's death. The king maintains that all these matters trouble him deeply.

A messenger enters, warning Claudius that Laertes and a band of followers have overcome their soldiers and are on the way to the palace. He says that many of the common people have been proclaiming Laertes the new king of Denmark. Indignant, Gertrude says they are like hunting dogs blindly following a false trail.

3. Laertes Confronts Claudius

Laertes bursts in, insulting Claudius and demanding he return his father. Gertrude tries to restrain Laertes, but he ignores her, refusing to calm down. Assuring Gertrude that he has no fear, Claudius asks Laertes to explain why he is so upset.

Laertes demands to know the circumstances of Polonius's death. He threatens immediate revenge against his killer. There is quite a contrast between Laertes' approach to vengeance and Hamlet's. However, the difference is not just a matter of temperament. The circumstances of Polonius's death are much clearer than those of Old Hamlet's.

Claudius tells Laertes that no one will stand in his way, but mentions the need to establish who was actually responsible for his father's death. As the king assures Laertes that he is in no way implicated, Ophelia reappears.

4. A Mind Truly O'erthrown

Laertes is greatly distressed at his sister's mental state. When Ophelia begins to sing lines appearing to relate to the funeral of their father, Laertes becomes more strongly motivated to seek revenge.

Ophelia distributes flowers to those present. She gives Laertes rosemary for remembrance and pansies for thoughts. Claudius gets fennel and columbines, associated with, respectively, flattery and thanklessness. For Gertrude, it's rue (for sorrow) and a daisy (a false heart). Ophelia tells Gertrude that she would have given her violets (faithfulness), had they not withered when Polonius died. For herself, it's rue only. Ophelia is showing both shrewd insight into character and a delicate sense of irony.

She ends with a touching song of mourning for her father.

5. Claudius Wins Laertes Over

After Ophelia leaves, Claudius speaks brief words of comfort to Laertes. He proposes that the young man appoint a group of friends to witness and judge a discussion between himself and Laertes regarding the death of Polonius. Claudius says he would sacrifice his life, his kingdom, and all his worldly goods if Laertes' friends find him involved in any way.

Laertes accepts the proposal, insisting the discussion deal with his father's circumscribed burial rites. Claudius promises a full explanation. He assures Laertes that Polonius's killer will suffer severe punishment.

Act IV, Scene 6 HORATIO HEARS FROM HAMLET

A sailor approaches Horatio, handing him a letter from Hamlet (referred to here as "the ambassador"). It contains details of how the Danish ship bound for England was attacked by pirates, whose ship Hamlet was able to leap onto in order to return to Denmark.

The letter asks Horatio to help the sailor and his mates get access to Claudius, for whom they also bear letters. After reading the letter, Horatio sends the men to Claudius, telling them to come back quickly to take him to Hamlet. The letter had mentioned important and startling news, much of which concerns Rosencrantz and Guildenstern.

Act IV, Scene 7 CLAUDIUS AND LAERTES

1. Claudius Continues to Work on Laertes

Claudius has convinced Laertes that Hamlet was responsible for Polonius's death. The king states that Hamlet also plotted against his own life. It's not clear whether this is factual. Gertrude may have told the king that Hamlet thought he was hidden behind the arras. Claudius may be fabricating, or perhaps he regards *The Murder of Gonzago* as a threat against his life.

Laertes asks why Claudius did not act directly against Hamlet. Apparently he does not know about the purpose of the mission to England. The king gives two reasons. The first is that Hamlet is very dear to Gertrude. The second is the high esteem in which the common people hold the prince. Claudius says punishing Hamlet might have produced a strong reaction from them.

Satisfied only in part, Laertes complains that because of Hamlet his father is dead and Ophelia has lost her mind. He looks forward, however, to vengeance. Claudius consoles Laertes, promising action against Hamlet soon enough.

2. Claudius Hears From Hamlet

A messenger brings in letters for Claudius and Gertrude delivered by the sailors. Claudius reads his aloud. In it, Hamlet indicates he will visit Claudius the next day to explain his return to Denmark.

Losing composure, the king thinks he is being deceived. He assures himself, however, that the handwriting is Hamlet's. He turns to Laertes for advice. All the young man can offer is an eagerness to confront Hamlet.

3. Claudius and Laertes Plot Against Hamlet

Impressed with Laertes' reaction, Claudius asks if he will follow his lead. Laertes agrees as long as he will not be denied vengeance. Claudius speaks of a plan to bring about Hamlet's death as if by accident.

Laertes asks for an active part. Claudius agrees. He mentions that when Hamlet heard Laertes' reputation as a swordsman given high praise by a recent visitor from France. he became so jealous he could hardly wait to challenge Laertes to a fencing match.

The king breaks off abruptly. Calling into question the strength of Laertes' love for his father, he observes that, unless acted upon speedily, good intentions often wither and die. Claudius needs to be convinced Laertes is fully committed to killing Hamlet. When Claudius asks how serious he is, Laertes says he would go so far as to slash Hamlet's throat in church.

Claudius seems reassured. He suggests Laertes lie low until he (Claudius) can lure the prince into a fencing match in which Laertes will use an unblunted sword to run Hamlet through. Laertes approves, suggesting he'll dip the sword point in a deadly poison. Perhaps he has doubts about killing Hamlet by swordsmanship alone. Claudius appears agreeable, but suggests that should these measures fail, he will have a cup of poisoned wine prepared for Hamlet to drink from during a break in the match.

Such treachery is typical of Claudius. Laertes' resorting to poison reveals a different side of his character. His concern for Ophelia before departing for France and his bold storming of Claudius's palace notwithstanding, he now appears as corrupt as the king. It apparently fails to occur to either of them that a death caused by poison would hardly appear accidental. They seem overeager to have Hamlet die.

4. Gertrude Brings More Bad News

The queen interrupts the plotting, reporting that the body of Ophelia has been found floating in a nearby brook. Gertrude says she had been hanging garlands of flowers in a willow tree when a branch gave way. Her clothes buoyed her up for a time but she made no attempt to save herself. With religious songs on her lips, she sank to her death.

Gertrude's account is beautifully expressed, moving Laertes to tears, which he struggles to suppress. Excusing himself, he promises to speak fiery words once he has overcome his grief, then hurries away.

As with Polonius, Claudius utters no words of sorrow over Ophelia's death. Worried about keeping Laertes' rage in check, he urges the queen to follow as he pursues the young man.

ACT FIVE

Act V, Scene 1 THE FUNERAL OF OPHELIA

1. An Interlude of Morbid Humour

The two Clowns preparing Ophelia's grave argue about whether her remains deserve to be buried in sanctified ground, since it appears she took her own life. After bandying about a few legal terms, the two men agree Ophelia's corpse will receive a Christian burial because of the high station she held in life.

They go on to jest about how well established their profession is and how well their work stands the test of time. The First Clown argues that grave-digging dates back to the time of Adam. He also maintains that graves outlast structures made by any of the building trades.

While he labours on, the First Clown sends his partner to bring refreshments.

2. Hamlet and the Gravedigger

Hamlet and Horatio approach the gravesite from a distance. Hamlet comments on how unseemly it is for the gravemaker to be singing while he works. He also remarks about how carelessly the man treats the bones he keeps turning up.

Hamlet uses this occasion to reflect on the impermanence of human existence. He says that in their graves, those who were important and influential in life, such as politicians, aristocrats, lawyers, and land speculators, lose all their former lustre.

After asking whose grave this is, Hamlet gets into a battle of wits with the gravemaker, who more than holds his own. When the man unearths the skull of Yorick, a former court jester, Hamlet recalls happy times with Yorick. He observes that even masters of the world like Julius Caesar or Alexander the Great end up ashes and dust. He seems preoccupied with the futility of human life.

3. Hamlet vs. Laertes

Hamlet and Horatio observe in the distance a funeral procession that includes the king and queen. Hamlet notices that the deceased is not being given full rites, indicating that the person, obviously of high station, has committed suicide. He and Horatio move to one side and watch the proceedings unseen.

They overhear the clergyman explaining to an insistent Laertes the reasons for the foreshortened ceremony. In an officious manner, the priest states that because the circumstances of Ophelia's death are suspect, her body would not be receiving any of the forms of Christian burial had the king not ordered it. Laertes responds angrily, telling the priest that when he's burning in hell, Ophelia will rank high among the angels.

Gertrude speaks kindly of Ophelia, expressing the hope that she and Hamlet would have married. Mention of the prince's name triggers an angry outburst from Laertes. Leaping into the grave, he embraces his sister, calling for himself to be buried alive with her under a mound of earth as high as a mountain.

Hamlet is distressed over Ophelia's death and takes exception to Laertes' ranting. When he leaps into the grave, Laertes attempts to strangle him, but others quickly intervene. Hamlet challenges Laertes about which of them loved Ophelia more and criticizes him for his excessive speech.

The queen comes to Hamlet's defense, attributing his behaviour to his madness. As the prince stalks away, Claudius sends Horatio after him. In an aside, the king reminds Laertes that his opportunity for revenge is soon to come. He urges Gertrude to keep Hamlet under close observation.

Claudius promises to provide a "living monument" for Ophelia's grave, presumably a statue of her as she was in life.

Act V, Scene 2 RESOLUTION

1. Hard Evidence Against the King

In a corridor in the royal castle, Hamlet tells Horatio that during one sleepless night aboard the ship bound for England, he made a spur of the moment decision to enter by stealth the cabin occupied by Rosencrantz and Guildenstern. There he was able to obtain undetected the packet of letters they had brought from Denmark.

Hamlet speaks glowingly of impulsive acts, indicating that they can be highly successful on occasions when carefully planned action would fall short. He takes comfort in the belief that, no matter how awry our plans may go, God finds ways to guide us.

Hamlet reveals that one of the letters contained an instruction to the English authorities to have him beheaded. He hands Horatio the letter so he can see for himself. Hamlet says that upon learning of Claudius's intention, he was inspired to write a new commission, which ordered the deaths of Rosencrantz and Guildenstern. Sealing the letter with a royal signet he happened to have in his purse, Hamlet put it in his companions' cabin along with the other letters. On the next day, the pirates attacked, creating his opportunity to return to Denmark.

When Horatio appears to question the fate of Rosencrantz and Guildenstern, Hamlet says it was no worse than they deserved, since they willingly did the bidding of the king. This sounds extreme. Rosencrantz and Guildenstern were certainly the king's men, but there is no evidence they were aware of the full purpose of their mission. Hamlet assures his friend that his conscience is clear.

Having read the letter, Horatio condemns Claudius's behavior. Hamlet asks if the sum of the king's sins—killing Old Hamlet, seducing

Gertrude, cheating him of his right to the throne, plotting against his life—isn't more than sufficient to justify striking against him.

Horatio avoids a direct response, pointing out instead that Claudius will soon learn the fate of Rosencrantz and Guildenstern. He seems to be urging Hamlet to act quickly. The prince agrees that the time is short but deems it more than sufficient.

Hamlet expresses regret over his treatment of Laertes at the gravesite. Because they have suffered similar losses, he promises to make amends. However, he takes exception again to Laertes' excessive words of grief.

2. A Sporting Proposition

Osric, a well-to-do henchman of Claudius and a man given to great affectation of speech, dress, and manners, comes on behalf of the king. He tells Hamlet that Claudius is prepared to make a considerable wager on his skills in a fencing match with Laertes. All that remains is for Hamlet to consent to take part.

Hamlet and Horatio make great sport of Osric, who is so obtuse he fails to understand he is being ridiculed. Hamlet mocks Osric's manner of speech but does agree to participate in the match.

Once Osric leaves, a more plain-spoken courtier (a lord) asks if Hamlet is willing to begin straightaway. The prince gives ready consent. As he is about to leave, the lord informs Hamlet that Gertrude wants him to treat Laertes kindly before the match begins. The prince is agreeable.

When they are alone, Horatio suggests that Hamlet will probably lose. The prince disagrees, indicating that, since Laertes' departure for France, he has been practising his skills with the rapier regularly.

Momentarily sick at heart, Hamlet soon recovers, dismissing the feeling as womanish. Wondering if the prince is mentally ready to fight, Horatio offers to arrange a postponement.

Hamlet declines, maintaining that what will be, will be. The best one can do, he believes, is be prepared for any outcome, even an early death.

3. The Preliminaries

Claudius places Laertes' hand in Hamlet's. The prince asks the young man to forgive his hurtful behaviour. He says his diseased mind was responsible for it and that, in a way, he is as much a victim of his madness as Laertes.

Laertes replies that he is satisfied for now with Hamlet's apology. However, he says he needs the approval a panel of experts on honour in order to settle the matter fully. In the meantime, he will take Hamlet at his word. The prince responds positively, suggesting they begin the match.

This exchange is blatantly hypocritical. Hamlet knows full well that he was never truly insane. Laertes knows that he is about to try to kill Hamlet. It's as though they are engaging in verbal fencing before the actual swordplay.

In a modest-sounding remark, Hamlet implies that Laertes' skills as a swordsman far outshine his own. Laertes accuses him of mockery. He's not far wrong. Hamlet had told Horatio earlier that he expected to "win at the odds."

Turning to Claudius, however, Hamlet says that, despite the odds, the king will lose his wager. Again the prince affects modesty. Claudius assures him that he believes Hamlet will win.

During the selection of weapons, Laertes is careful to obtain the unblunted sword. Hamlet selects his weapon rather carelessly.

Claudius orders large cups filled with wine so he can toast Hamlet if he does well in the early going. Into the cup he will drink from, Claudius promises to drop a valuable pearl as a reward for Hamlet. He then declares the match open.

4. The Main Event

Hamlet scores the first hit. Laertes disputes it but is overruled by Osric. Claudius stops the competition for a moment. After taking a drink, he drops the pearl into the cup, which he offers Hamlet. It is actually hollow and contains poison. Hamlet orders the cup set aside, however, preferring to finish the match.

When the fight resumes, Hamlet scores another hit. As the opponents rest, Gertrude hands Hamlet a napkin to wipe his brow. Then she raises the cup containing the pearl to her own lips.

Claudius tries to stop her, but she insists on drinking. The queen offers the cup to Hamlet, who declines again. Gertrude wipes perspiration from her son's face.

With Hamlet off guard, Laertes tells Claudius that he'll strike with the envenomed sword. The king overrules him. Laertes admits in an aside to having qualms of conscience at this thought.

Flushed with success, Hamlet urges Laertes to play the next bout. The prince accuses him of holding back. Laertes responds angrily. They fight on, neither registering a hit.

During a pause for breath, Laertes wounds Hamlet when his back is turned. The men scuffle, each picking up the other's weapon. Hamlet stabs Laertes.

Gertrude collapses. About to die, she warns Hamlet that the wine is poisoned.

Laertes tells Hamlet they are soon to die. He confirms that Gertrude has drunk poison, and blames Claudius for the treachery.

Free at last to act, Hamlet stabs the king with the poisoned sword and pours poisoned wine down his throat. Claudius dies calling for help.

About to die, Laertes begs Hamlet's forgiveness. The prince tells him to seek absolution from heaven.

5. The Aftermath

Hamlet regrets that there is no time to tell his story publicly. He leaves that task to Horatio, who seizes the poisoned cup and tries to drink from it. Hamlet manages to wrest it from him.

Meanwhile the army of Young Fortinbras arrives at the palace, returning successfully from the campaign in Poland. The ambassadors from England arrive to report on the deaths of Rosencrantz and Guildenstern. Osric says that the forces of Fortinbras saw fit to fire a volley at the ambassadors.

Introduction to Hamlet

Hamlet regrets the lack of time to hear of the deaths of his former friends. With his dying breath, he endorses Fortinbras as next king of Denmark.

6. Fortinbras Assumes Power

Fortinbras marvels at the number of corpses he sees. The English ambassadors agree that the sight is "dismal," but are upset that they cannot report to Claudius. They hoped to be appropriately thanked.

Horatio tells the ambassadors that Claudius would hardly have welcomed their news. He urges Fortinbras and the ambassadors to have the corpses put on public display, where he can tell the whole story to the people of Denmark.

Sorrowful over what has happened, Fortinbras nonetheless lays claim to power in Denmark. The "rights of memory" he refers to may have been part of the agreement that governed the duel fought by his father and Old Hamlet. It may also be that Fortinbras is being opportunistic.

Fortinbras orders appropriate military rites and ceremony accorded the corpse of Hamlet. He speaks most respectfully of the dead prince, deploring again the many deaths that have occurred. His soldiers bear the bodies away. Ceremonial gunfire is heard.

part two

suit the action to the word, the word to the action

Introduction to the Essays

This section features four essays on important themes in *Hamlet*. They are included in this volume for two reasons. The first is to serve as models for students. The other is to provide material intended to deepen understanding of the play and stimulate thinking about it.

Ideas for literary essays often occur when we pay close attention to a work under study. Reflecting upon it, we discover aspects that pique our curiosity. We wonder for instance about the scene in which Polonius sends his servant Reynaldo to spy on Laertes in France. That mission is never mentioned again, so why is there so much detail?

Although sensitive to Hamlet's difficulties in avenging his father's murder, we see him at times as a cruel and callous person. Claudius is certainly villainous, but he is also not without appealing qualities. These discrepancies raise questions worth considering.

As he tells Horatio about his escape from the ship bound for England, Hamlet praises rash actions and divine intervention. Before fighting the duel with Laertes, he speaks of the determining effects of "a special providence." Because these appear to be assumptions rather than facts, they invite looking into.

From time to time, Hamlet displays an overly negative attitude toward the two women in the play. Although we can understand Hamlet's reasons, we wonder how truly Gertrude and Ophelia deserve mistreatment from the prince.

These observations contain the germ for the essays that follow. All began with the discovery of matters of interest in *Hamlet*. No claim is made for the essays as works of original scholarship. Nothing in them however has been knowingly borrowed.

The title of the first essay is "A Fetch of Warrant: The Indirect Method in *Hamlet*." Polonius calls his indirect method a "fetch of warrant," which means a strategy highly likely to succeed. His strong commitment to roundabout methods led to a search for examples over the course of the play. Polonius and Claudius use indirect methods twice when testing the theory that Hamlet's apparent madness is owing to the loss of his relationship with Ophelia. Neither attempt was successful, and the latter cost Polonius his life

These results gave rise to another possibility: that in *Hamlet*, indirect methods are both ineffective and potentially dangerous. A close analysis of other events and situations indicated that almost every use of an indirect approach failed. The evidence is documented in "A Fetch of Warrant."

The second essay, "Mighty Opposites: The Virtues of Claudius, The Vices of Hamlet," came to mind from Hamlet's remark to Horatio that Rosencrantz and Guildenstern got caught in a struggle between two "mighty opposites," himself and Claudius. Our initial reaction is to feel sympathy for Hamlet and disgust with Claudius. Those feelings become nuanced when we reflect further.

In addition to causing the deaths of Rosencrantz and Guildenstern, Hamlet treats Ophelia harshly in her sewing room and much worse during the nunnery scene. Although Claudius murdered his brother, he does express sincere remorse twice in soliloquy. He also faces down an angry Laertes who has him and Gertrude at his mercy. Neither man is fully what he seems. These reflections led to an exploration of the appealing side of Claudius and the offensive side of Hamlet.

The third essay is entitled "Defying Augury: God, Fate, Freewill, and Chance in *Hamlet*." When Hamlet feels momentary sickness of heart after agreeing to the duel with Laertes, Horatio offers to arrange a postponement. Hamlet recovers quickly, saying "we defy augury." He is prepared to let matters unfold as they will. After aborting the voyage to England, Hamlet speaks of a "divinity that shapes our ends."

These are his first statements about what motivates or determines human behaviour. Because they come late in the play, it seems fitting to test their validity over its entirety. That is what "Defying Augury" attempts.

The final essay is "Frailty, Is Woman Thy True Name?" Heartbroken over his mother's decision to marry Claudius so soon after the death of his father, Hamlet cries out in soliloquy, "Frailty, thy name is woman!" He appears to believe that his mother is subject to a fault inherent in women. This statement raises several questions. How frail is Gertrude? How frail is Ophelia? And what about womankind? The essay looks for answers.

A Fetch of Warrant
The Indirect Method in Hamlet

As Polonius is about to send his servant Reynaldo to spy on Laertes in Paris, he explains his preferred method for securing information or confirming suspicions. What he tells Reynaldo in part is:

> *Your bait of falsehood takes this carp of truth;*
> *And thus do we of wisdom and of reach,*
> *With windlasses, and with assays of bias,*
> *By indirections find directions out.* (ii, i, 63-66)

In plainer English, Polonius is saying that when angling after truth, if you bait your hook with false information, you often wind up catching a big fish. Putting it another way, he maintains that by making roundabout approaches (windlasses) or following a curving path (a bias) rather than a straight line, you can discover the truth or accomplish something meaningful more readily than by proceeding in a direct, forthright manner.

Before Reynaldo departs for France, Polonius gives him specific instructions on how to apply this method. We never hear of him again and are left to wonder about how well the indirect method might have worked. With that in mind, however, we can turn to the remainder of the play, which abounds in examples of the indirect approach. Think of Polonius when he attempts to prove that Hamlet's madness stems from frustrated love. Of Claudius and Gertrude when they put Rosencrantz and Guildenstern up to spying on Hamlet. Of Claudius when he plots to have the English king execute Hamlet. Of Claudius and Laertes when they scheme to bring about Hamlet's death in a fencing match. And of Hamlet himself when he decides to stage *The Murder of Gonzago.*

With so many instances of indirection in the play, it seems reasonable to regard the action in *Hamlet* as a sustained inquiry into its usefulness. Our curiosity about the success of Reynaldo's mission, a minor matter to be sure, is easily applied to these other undertakings. When we hear of them, each seems plausible, and we wonder how they will turn out. Furthermore, each is of considerable significance, if not crucial, to plot development. It is in fact no exaggeration to say that as the indirect method goes, so goes the play.

***

Polonius is first to employ the indirect method. After hearing Ophelia's account of Hamlet's disturbing visit to her sewing room, Polonius concludes that thwarted love for Ophelia is the cause of Hamlet's lunacy. When he presents this idea to Claudius and Gertrude, the king is not fully convinced. Polonius proposes that he and Claudius secretly observe an interview between Hamlet and Ophelia. He assures the king that this theory will be proved beyond doubt.

When they meet in the nunnery scene, however, Hamlet tells Ophelia in one breath that he once loved her and in the next denies that he ever did. Haranguing her over the wantonness of women and the knavery of men, he urges her never to marry or if she must, that she be sure to wed a fool.

Although harsh and bitter, these remarks are coherent and hardly the ravings of a lunatic. Claudius insists that Hamlet is sane enough. He rejects the notion of any connection between Hamlet's deranged behaviour and thwarted love. The king tells Polonius that Hamlet is more dangerous than insane, and resolves to send him to England on state business. Claudius hopes a change of scene will improve the prince's mood.

Hamlet's denial that he has ever loved Ophelia convinces Claudius that love is not the cause of his objectionable behaviour. We know, however, from the prince's letter to Ophelia, which Polonius read to the king and queen, that Hamlet's love is steadfast and deep. Perhaps that is what prompts Polonius to propose a further testing of his theory.

He tells Claudius that he will arrange an interview between Hamlet and his mother in her chambers after the performance of *The Murder of Gonzago*. Polonius says he will instruct the queen to be direct with him, hoping that would persuade Hamlet to speak his mind. All the while, Polonius will be hidden behind an arras, able to overhear everything. Approving the plan, Claudius stresses the need to keep Hamlet under close observation.

When the play ends prematurely, Hamlet visits the queen's apartment. He confronts Gertrude aggressively. Afraid for her life, she cries out for help. Polonius joins the outcry from behind the arras. Mistaking him for Claudius, Hamlet runs his sword through the arras, killing the old man.

Not only does Polonius fail to prove his point, he dies in the attempt. In the conversation between Hamlet and Gertrude that follows, no mention is made of Ophelia. The indirect method is unavailing.

***

Claudius and Gertrude use an indirect approach when they invite Rosencrantz and Guildenstern to Elsinore to try to determine the cause of Hamlet's apparent lunacy.

Despite their willingness to cooperate, Rosencrantz and Guildenstern are unsuccessful almost from the beginning in their efforts to draw Hamlet out. When first encountering them, the prince suspects their motives and forces them to admit that their visit is at the behest of the king and queen. Hamlet tells Rosencrantz and Guildenstern that they are most unlikely to find anything worth reporting to Claudius and Gertrude. He does, however, make a remark about being mad "north-north-west." The significance is apparently lost on his companions. They offer no comment, and there is no evidence that the king and queen hear of it.

When Rosencrantz and Guildenstern report to Claudius and Gertrude, they confess that Hamlet's "crafty madness" is keeping them at arm's length. They do report that Hamlet's mood improved considerably with the arrival of the travelling players. When they tell Claudius that Hamlet has scheduled a performance on the next night, the king responds positively, little realizing it contains a trap.

Once the trap is sprung, Rosencrantz and Guildenstern function fully as agents of the king. They try to get Hamlet to calm himself and consent to visit Gertrude in her apartment. When Guildenstern asks Hamlet to reveal the cause of his "distemper," the prince rebuffs him and goes to meet Gertrude.

After the death of Polonius, Claudius sends Rosencrantz and Guildenstern in search of the old man's body. Rosencrantz tells Claudius that Hamlet is under guard and will not cooperate. When Guildenstern brings Hamlet to Claudius, the prince treats the king disrespectfully but does reveal that the body is under a staircase. The indirect method fails again.

***

Claudius focuses now on the threat the prince poses. His plan to deal with it is indirect. Rosencrantz and Guildenstern will again be his agents. They are to supervise Hamlet on the mission to England that Claudius had spoken of earlier. Its purpose is greatly changed. The English authorities are to put Hamlet to death as soon as he arrives.

More eager than ever to assist the king, Rosencrantz and Guildenstern get Hamlet aboard ship. Though the blame is hardly theirs, the prince never arrives in England. As he reveals later to

Horatio, Hamlet stole into their cabin and removed the packet of letters they were carrying. Discovering Claudius's order to have him killed, Hamlet wrote a new commission instructing the English authorities to execute his former friends. The next day Hamlet jumped aboard an attacking pirate ship that returned him to Denmark.

The indirect method again proves fruitless. Rosencrantz and Guildenstern journey on toward death, a fate not entirely undeserved given their servile natures. Claudius is left to deal with his difficult nephew, who is more wary and dangerous than ever.

***

Claudius adopts another indirect method to try to bring about Hamlet's death, When Laertes returns from France bent on avenging the killing of Polonius, the king plots with him to have Hamlet killed in an apparent accident. Claudius suggests they lure the prince into a fencing match in which Laertes would run him through with a sword left unblunted. Laertes wants the sword tip dipped in a venom for which there is no antidote. As a further measure, Claudius decides to poison a cup of wine to be offered Hamlet if necessary during an interval in the fighting.

The plan is hastily conceived. Laertes may or may not be the better swordsman. Hamlet's death would hardly appear accidental if he were poisoned. The scheme does, however, begin to unfold as planned. Hamlet agrees to take part and does not bother to examine Laertes' foil.

But as the match progresses, matters slip out of control. Hamlet prevails in the fighting. Laertes wounds him with the poisoned tip. In the ensuing scuffle, Hamlet seizes Laertes' sword and wounds him. Gertrude has drunk the poisoned wine. With his last breath, Laertes blames the king. Hamlet kills Claudius. Young Fortinbras arrives in time to take over the Danish throne.

The indirect approach is completely ineffective.

***

The case against the indirect method seems strong. There is one instance, however, in which it may have achieved a measure of success: Hamlet's decision to stage the play-within-the-play.

The idea occurs to him after the arrival of the travelling actors. The prince is impressed with the emotion with which the First Player recites a passage describing Hecuba's mourning of her husband's death. Hamlet decides to have a play performed before the whole court. The company will present *The Murder of Gonzago*, a tragedy to which Hamlet will add lines of his own. Hamlet reasons that the ghost's story could be a fabrication. He decides to test it by incorporating into the play some of the circumstances of Old Hamlet's death as reported by the ghost. If Claudius gives even the slightest indication of bad conscience, Hamlet says the ghost's story will be confirmed and he'll know what he needs to do.

This plan appears sound. The information Hamlet has is hearsay. It is hard to know how far to trust the word of a ghost. Hamlet's meeting with the ghost was private. No witness could confirm the story if Hamlet were to kill Claudius.

Nonetheless, the wisdom of staging the modified version of *The Murder of Gonzago* is questionable. Regardless of how Claudius may react, Hamlet will have revealed his suspicions. There is, however, no guarantee of evidence of guilt. By tipping his hand, Hamlet would be certain to experience reaction from Claudius. The stakes are high. There is no hard evidence against the king. Hamlet needs a confession of guilt. The likelihood is uncertain.

The king reacts in a startled, angry, and possibly incriminating manner when Lucianus pours poison into the ear of the Player King. Claudius calls for torches to be lit, then retires to his chambers. Hamlet's immediate response is manic. He breaks into wild and whirling words intended to make sport of Claudius. He tells Horatio that he is prepared to take the ghost at his word. Hamlet appears convinced of the king's guilt.

An enraged Claudius prepares to send Hamlet immediately to England. The prince makes matters much worse by killing Polonius. Claudius orders his execution upon arrival in England.

It's unclear how motivated Hamlet really is to kill the king. He had an opportunity when stumbling upon Claudius trying to pray, which he passed up because he thinks he would be sending the king's soul to heaven. Hamlet's indirect approach to establishing Claudius's guilt has left him worse off than ever. Unable to strike at Claudius, Hamlet is being sent to England on a journey he seems content to undertake.

The prince's attitude toward the voyage is puzzling. He had already told his mother that the trip was an opportunity for Rosencrantz and Guildenstern to "marshal [him] to knavery." When he discovers his death warrant on the ship, Hamlet writes a new one ordering the deaths of his former friends. A chance encounter with a pirate ship gets him back to Denmark. It's hard to understand why he sends the king a letter announcing his return. It gives Claudius time to react. Hamlet appears to be placing obstacles in his own path. He possesses a warrant ordering his death. It alone might justify acting against the king.

More on guard than ever, Claudius plots Hamlet's death again. That scheme misfires. Hamlet gets revenge at an enormous cost. A more direct approach would have served him better. Killing Claudius might have cost only his own life.

***

In every case, indirect methods prove futile. The forbidden love theory was never validated. Rosencrantz and Guildenstern gained no insights into Hamlet's behaviour. Claudius's attempts to protect himself from Hamlet came to nothing. The play-within-the-play gave Hamlet private confirmation of Claudius's guilt, but the king's death resulted more from the unravelling of the plan to have Hamlet die than from any initiative on the prince's part.

The indirect method might have worked well enough for Reynaldo on his mission to spy on Laertes. What is certain is that every character in the play who employed or was party to an indirect approach met a violent end, sometimes deservedly, more often not. Direct action could hardly have produced worse results.

Mighty Opposites
The Virtues of Claudius, The Vices of Hamlet

Our first impression of Claudius is one of contempt. He has seduced his brother's wife, murdered his brother, succeeded him as king, and married his widow. We feel compassion for Hamlet. His father's ghost tells him of the murder and demands revenge, but leaves it to him to find a way of achieving it. The prince is obliged to kill a man he already despises who is now the monarch. Lacking evidence, he stages a play he hopes will induce Claudius to confess his crime. The king reacts by taking measures against the prince that result in both their deaths. Hamlet looks like a victim. He gets vengeance but at the cost of his own life. Claudius is punished for his crime, but many others die as well.

The prince is not entirely a victim. He tells Horatio after escaping from the ship bound for England that he sent Rosencrantz and Guildenstern on to their deaths. Hamlet says they should have known better than to get involved in a clash between "mighty opposites," himself and Claudius. The king is not entirely bad. A closer look at the play reveals that Claudius displays from time to time characteristics that are not without considerable appeal. Though we may laugh at Hamlet's sardonic wit and marvel at his skill with the sword, his behaviour on many occasions leaves much to be desired. Before deciding where our sympathies and censure lie, we need to examine the mighty opposites in detail.

I. HAMLET AND CLAUDIUS

One way to consider character differences between Claudius and Hamlet is to observe them closely when they are together. In the play's second scene the king is in the limelight. Hamlet plays a more minor role. Claudius explains the need for the quick marriage to Gertrude. He speaks of a plan to counter a threatened invasion from Norway. After approving Laertes' petition to return to France, Claudius reaches out to Hamlet. He commends him for the respect he shows the memory of his father, but reproves the prince for carrying this "filial obligation" too far. Encouraging Hamlet to think of him as a surrogate father, Claudius proclaims his nephew heir to the throne. He says his feelings for Hamlet are those of the most devoted of natural fathers.

The king is showing poise and confidence. Although Claudius opposes Hamlet's wish to return to university in Wittenberg, he wants to have the prince near him as a beloved family member and the foremost figure in court. When Hamlet's says he will follow his mother's wishes, Claudius pronounces his words "a loving and a fair reply."

Hamlet is barely civil throughout this scene. His words in an aside, "A little more than kin and less than kind," reflect his low opinion of Claudius. When Gertrude asks that he cease mourning for his father and look with a kinder eye on Claudius, Hamlet faults her for implying that he only seems to be grieving. He makes clear that, far from affecting the forms of mourning, he feels genuine grief. These remarks are likely a criticism of the queen for not grieving the death of Old Hamlet sufficiently.

In soliloquy, Hamlet reveals his true feelings for both Claudius and Gertrude. His complaint that their wedding occurred too soon after his father's funeral is valid enough, but his negative attitude toward Claudius bears examination. He refers to Claudius as a lecherous beast and likens Old Hamlet to a sun god. He says the difference between his father and Claudius exceeded that between himself and Hercules. These comparisons are excessive. Old Hamlet may well have been, as Hamlet maintains, kind and considerate toward Gertrude.

Horatio had already mentioned the old king's prowess in battle, and later calls him a "goodly king." Yet when Hamlet first encounters his father's ghost, it admits to having committed a number of "foul crimes" for which it is condemned to burn in hellfire. This seems hardly the fate of a sun god.

It may well be that Old Hamlet was the better man. Despite the strengths Claudius has shown in this scene, he remains an adulterous murderer. In the soliloquy, however, Hamlet is judging the two brothers prior to his interview with the ghost. It is difficult to understand his aversion to Claudius at that point. It's also not clear why he holds such an idealized view of his father.

In this scene we note a cordial, tolerant, generous side of the king, and sullen, bitter, petulant traits in Hamlet. The king's attempts to reach out to Hamlet sound genuine. The prince's attitude toward his uncle contains a bias that seems hard to justify. Claudius looks rather good, Hamlet less so.

***

In the nunnery scene, Hamlet treats Ophelia harshly and inveighs against women in general. Claudius and Polonius observe them in secret. They are testing Polonius's theory that the loss of Hamlet's relationship with Ophelia has caused the prince's apparent madness.

After witnessing Hamlet's tirade, Claudius rejects Polonius's theory. He says that the prince's words, though somewhat disordered, are those of a troubled person who could prove dangerous. The king considers sending Hamlet on a mission to England, thinking a change of scene might improve his mood.

Claudius is both shrewd and decisive. He realizes Hamlet poses a threat he must deal with. When Polonius presses for one more testing, the king agrees, stressing the need to monitor "madness in great ones." Although Claudius appears concerned about Hamlet's mental health, he recognizes that the prince could become dangerous, and that whatever is troubling him is no small matter.

Hamlet's behaviour is disgraceful. His attack against women likely reflects his disgust with Gertrude for marrying Claudius. His scathing treatment of Ophelia is doubtless owing to the breaking off of their relationship. His distress is understandable, his behaviour deplorable. He does little to engage our sympathies. Hamlet is now at greater disadvantage in his quest for revenge. The king is becoming wary of him.

***

Hamlet and Claudius meet briefly before the performance of *The Murder of Gonzago*. When the king asks Hamlet how he "fares," Hamlet puns on the word, telling Claudius that, like a chameleon, he eats the air. He compares himself to a capon, a castrated cock being fattened up for slaughter. These remarks probably indicate how Hamlet views himself vis-à-vis the king: as someone being set up to be killed. Whatever their significance, the words are lost on Claudius.

During a pause in the performance, Claudius asks Hamlet if the play contains offensive material. The prince says it does, but assures the king that neither of them should be troubled because they each have a clear conscience. However, as poison is poured into the ear of the sleeping Player King, Claudius rushes to his chambers. Polonius orders the performance stopped. Hamlet celebrates the success of the trap he has sprung.

The conversations show contrasting attitudes in Hamlet and the king. Claudius's greeting shows interest in the prince's welfare. Hamlet responds by making puns and oblique references that are unintelligible. When Claudius asks about possible offence in the play, the question is civil enough. Hamlet's response is sardonic. The king is being polite. Hamlet speaks down to him.

The reenactment of the murder of Old Hamlet startles Claudius. Guildenstern tells Hamlet the king is "marvelous distempered." Claudius has been caught off guard. He recovers quickly, however, ordering Rosencrantz and Guildenstern to accompany Hamlet on the voyage to England. Hamlet is manic over his success, but agrees to go to his mother's chambers instead of confronting Claudius. The king takes direct action. Hamlet delays.

***

On his way to meet Gertrude, Hamlet encounters Claudius attempting to pray for forgiveness for killing Old Hamlet. Hamlet considers killing him but forbears because he believes the king's soul would go to heaven, whereas true vengeance requires that it go to hell. He sheathes his sword and goes to meet his mother. Hamlet's reason for moving on makes sense if Claudius truly is atoning for the murder. But as the king reveals after Hamlet has gone, his effort to pray failed. Hamlet had revenge within his grasp.

Claudius abandons his attempt at prayer because he is unwilling to give up the rewards the murder has brought him. Divine forgiveness is out of the question. He resolves to send Hamlet to England immediately. Hamlet assumes that dying at prayer would send Claudius's soul to heaven. It is difficult to believe that prayer alone could absolve anyone of a sin as great as a brother's murder. Hamlet's reluctance looks more like a failure of nerve. The king is being realistic and decisive. Hamlet is dragging his feet.

***

Hamlet is brought before Claudius after the killing of Polonius. The king demands to know where he has left the body. Hamlet answers in a roundabout manner, disrespectful of Polonius and insolent toward Claudius. Hamlet finally reveals that the body is under a staircase.

Claudius tells Hamlet that for his own safety he must depart immediately for England. Hamlet agrees, then runs off with Rosencrantz and Guildenstern in pursuit. In a short soliloquy Claudius says he plans to have Hamlet executed upon arrival in England.

The contrast between prince and king is strong. Claudius plans another killing to try to secure his hold on the throne. Hamlet chooses delay over dispatch, apparently content to undertake a voyage the purpose of which, as he told Gertrude, is to "marshall [him] to knavery." It would also postpone the avenging of Old Hamlet's death.

Claudius's steadfastness of purpose would be admirable if it were evident under honourable circumstances. We understand Hamlet's reluctance, probably on moral grounds, to murder his uncle for the sake of vengeance. His apparent lack of remorse over killing Polonius, however, does not acquit him well.

***

Back from the aborted voyage to England, Hamlet informs Claudius by letter that he will soon arrive to explain his "sudden and more strange return." Claudius is taken aback but recovers quickly, plotting Hamlet's death with Laertes. The king sees what he needs to do. He and Laertes develop an elaborate plan to end Hamlet's life as if by accident.

It is difficult to see what advantage Hamlet gains in giving the king advance notice of his return. He possesses the warrant Claudius signed against his life. Why forewarn a deadly enemy? Moreover, the letter has a bitter, mocking tone that does not portray the prince as formidable and resolute. If this is more of the antic disposition, it's far too late, Hamlet must realize that his life is in great danger.

***

At Ophelia's funeral, Claudius intervenes when a shouting match and scuffle develop between Hamlet and Laertes. Claudius orders them separated, then joins Gertrude in attributing Hamlet's behaviour to his madness. When Hamlet stalks away, the king tells Horatio to pursue and look after him. He instructs Gertrude to keep Hamlet under close observation. In an aside, he reminds Laertes that he will soon have his revenge.

Hamlet's conduct is deplorable. In a rant he declares that his own love for Ophelia greatly exceeded that of Laertes. Claudius is under control and in command. Hamlet is out of control, publicly disgracing himself.

***

The final encounter between Hamlet and the king comes at the fencing match. Claudius begins by making peace between Hamlet and Laertes. As they select foils, the prince suggests with seeming modesty that Claudius may lose the wager he has placed on him to win. The king insists, however, that his bet is sure. He promises to drink to each success Hamlet has during the match.

When Hamlet wins the first bout, Claudius drinks from a wine cup into which he slips a pearl containing poison. He offers it to Hamlet, but the prince declines to drink until the match is over. When Hamlet scores the next point, Gertrude drinks from the cup. Claudius is powerless to intervene. Hamlet and Laertes fight to a draw. As they pause to rest, they each wound the other with the tip of the poisoned sword.

Gertrude collapses, telling Hamlet she's been poisoned. Claudius says her fall is the result of seeing the combatants bleed. The dying Laertes confesses all, laying blame on the king. Hamlet stabs Claudius with the poisoned sword. He pretends only to be wounded and cries for help. Hamlet pours poisoned wine down his throat.

Claudius has tried to manage and control proceedings, but becomes increasingly helpless as the plot unravels. On the point of death himself, the prince takes revenge, calling Claudius an "incestuous, murderous, damnèd Dane." It appears to require words from Laertes to spur him on. One wonders if he would have acted without them.

As the play ends, Hamlet is not triumphant or even relieved at having killed the king. His dying wishes are to have Horatio clear his wounded name and express support for Fortinbras to become king. A feckless Claudius pretends that Gertrude had only fainted and insists that he is only wounded after Hamlet stabs him. He has become a caricature of the man he appeared to be.

II. HAMLET AND OTHER CHARACTERS

Comparing the behaviour of Hamlet and Claudius when they interact is instructive enough, but hardly more than a good start. Another way of discovering significant character differences between them is to consider their relationships with other characters. We begin with the prince.

Hamlet and Ophelia

In spite of the love they apparently felt for each other, Hamlet's treatment of Ophelia is hardly indicative of tender feelings. One exception is in the letter Polonius reveals to Claudius and Gertrude, which reads in part, "that I love thee best, O most best! believe it." The other is the declaration at Ophelia's gravesite that his love exceeded that of forty thousand brothers.

Hamlet is anything but loving when he bursts into Ophelia's sewing room. She says he came in half-undressed, seizing her by the arm and staring at her. With a prolonged sigh, he released her and retreated from the room, his eyes upon her all the while. Ophelia says the visit greatly frightened her. Hamlet's actions are a dramatic example of the "antic disposition." He is doubtless also punishing Ophelia for breaking off their relationship.

In the nunnery scene Hamlet launches a scathing attack on women for their wanton behaviour and on men for being "arrant knaves." Turning harshly on Ophelia, he admits in one breath that he loved her but denies it in the next. He urges her to live in a nunnery, which for him likely means both convent and brothel. If Hamlet was trying to give convincing evidence of a mental disorder, he definitely has Ophelia persuaded. She pronounces him "blasted with ecstasy," and is genuinely saddened over his state of mind.

If Hamlet also intended to berate her for ending their relationship, that too was successful. He may not have known she was ordered to do it but even so, his attack on Ophelia does him little credit. She did not deserve the abuse.

***

During the preliminaries to *The Murder of Gonzago*, Hamlet declines his mother's invitation to join her. He lies at Ophelia's feet when she refuses his request to lie in her lap. He asks if she thought he had "country matters" in mind, and says what an appealing thought it is to "lie between maids' legs."

As the dumb-show begins. Hamlet assures Ophelia that the Prologue will make matters clear. He says the Prologue would be willing to interpret anything Ophelia might wish to show him. Hamlet tells her not to be ashamed of showing, because the speaker would feel no shame in revealing whatever it might mean. She tells the prince he is being disgusting.

Once the play is underway, Ophelia compliments Hamlet on the information he gives Claudius regarding the plot. He tells her that he could interpret between her and her lover if he could "see the puppets dangling." When she tells him his wit is keen, he says it would cost her a "groaning to take of [his] edge." She says that is even wittier but deplores the sexual innuendo.

When poison is poured in the ear of the sleeping Player King, Claudius rises, calling for light. Polonius orders the performance stopped. The spectators disperse.

Hamlet's treatment of Ophelia is unseemly. She finds his lewdness distasteful but fends it off politely. His intent is to make her feel uncomfortable, but less harshly than in the sewing room or the nunnery scene. Perhaps he has grown less angry with her. His remarks, however, take on a progressively sharper edge. We are impressed with Hamlet's nimble mind but share Ophelia's discomfort. This occasion is the last on which he sees Ophelia alive.

***

His hurtful influence increases exponentially when he kills Polonius. Hamlet expresses little regret and makes disparaging remarks about the old man. He shows no concern over the effects the death would have on his children. Polonius's death at the hands of the man she had loved makes Ophelia truly insane. In the presence of Claudius, Gertrude, and Laertes, she laments the death in a bizarre manner. Gertrude interrupts a conference between Claudius and Laertes later to report Ophelia's death by drowning. Hamlet's rash act caused Ophelia great suffering that led to an apparent suicide.

***

Hamlet and Horatio happen by chance upon Ophelia's funeral. Laertes berates the priest over her foreshortened burial rites and attacks Hamlet when the prince joins him in her grave. Hamlet rants at Laertes over his seemingly infinite love of his sister. Their behavior mars what should have been a solemn ceremony

Before Ophelia was forced to end their relationship, Hamlet cared deeply for her. At her funeral, he declares his love again. In the mean-time, however, his treatment of Ophelia became abusive apparently because he was unaware that she was ordered to break off with him. The consequences were disastrous and undeserved.

Hamlet and Gertrude

Early in the play, Hamlet is distant from his mother and Claudius. When Gertrude supports the king's desire that Hamlet cease mourning for his father and look more kindly upon him, Hamlet's rebuffs her. He says the "forms, modes, and shows of grief" apparent to her are nothing compared to the sorrow in his heart. He disapproves of Gertrude for insufficient mourning of Old Hamlet's death and her overly quick marriage to Claudius. In soliloquy, Hamlet blames her for disrespecting the memory of Old Hamlet. The prince considers

Claudius much inferior to his father. He finds it heartbreaking that Gertrude could stoop so low.

When Hamlet encounters his father's ghost, he learns that Claudius seduced her before he murdered Old Hamlet. The ghost speaks disapprovingly of Gertrude, but instructs Hamlet not to proceed against her. He is to leave her to heaven and her guilty conscience. After the ghost has gone, Hamlet calls his mother a "pernicious woman." He decides shortly to begin acting as if he were insane.

***

When Rosencrantz and Guildenstern arrive at the palace, Gertrude supports Claudius's request that they try to discover the cause of Hamlet's disordered behaviour. She promises a reward befitting a king if they are successful. Polonius comes to inform Claudius and the queen that he believes Hamlet's lunacy is owing to Ophelia's breaking off their relationship. When Claudius asks her opinion, Gertrude says it may be so. She tells Ophelia she hopes that restoration of their relationship will cure him.

The exchanges between Hamlet and Ophelia in the nunnery scene serve no such purpose. It does seem clear however that, as well as being supportive of Claudius, the queen is genuinely concerned for Hamlet. He wants even less to do with her because of her adultery with Claudius.

***

At the play-within-the-play begins, Hamlet declines Gertrude's invitation to sit with her in favour of joining Ophelia. When the Player Queen promises that she would never consider a second marriage, Hamlet's remark in an aside, "If she should break it now!" indicates that he has been watching Gertrude closely. When he asks her opinion of the play, the queen complains of the length of the Player Queen's remarks. Hamlet's response that she will keep her word sounds critical of Gertrude for remarrying so quickly.

Claudius's sudden decision to call off the performance causes Gertrude to summon Hamlet to her bedchamber. On his way he says that although his mood is murderous, he will only speak daggers to her.

The meeting begins with rancour. When the queen accuses Hamlet of offending Claudius, he tells her she has offended Old Hamlet. Gertrude says that he seems to have forgotten who she is. He replies that he knows her well enough and wishes she were not his mother. When the queen threatens to call the guards, Hamlet orders her to sit and hear some home truths about herself. Afraid for her life, Gertrude cries out. When Polonius responds, Hamlet thrusts his sword through the arras, believing he was killing Claudius. The queen calls the killing a "rash and bloody deed." Hamlet says it is almost as bad as killing a king and marrying his brother. He tells her to prepare to have her heart wrung.

Hamlet upbraids her for being blind to Claudius's faults. The queen takes his words to heart, admitting that her soul is spotted with sin. She begs him to stop, but he continues until his father's ghost intervenes. Gertrude thinks Hamlet is hallucinating. When the ghost has gone, he tells her he is as sane as she. Hamlet orders her to stop going to Claudius's bed and forbids her to reveal that he is mad only "in craft." The queen promises to obey. Hamlet's relationship with his mother has reached a turning point. She always had concerns for him, but her bond with Claudius has been strong. She is now becoming allied with her son. The change is evident immediately. When Claudius finds her in a state of anxiety, Gertrude tells him that in a fit of madness Hamlet has slain Polonius. Knowing full well that her son is sane, she says he weeps over what he has done, when in fact he showed almost no remorse.

***

After the quarrel between Hamlet and Laertes at Ophelia's funeral, the queen calls her son's behaviour "mere madness," which will soon pass. During a break in the fencing match, she notices Hamlet's shortness of breath. She drinks to his good luck from the poisoned cup and wipes sweat from Hamlet's face. The queen falls. With her dying breath, she warns Hamlet not to drink. Soon to die himself, Hamlet final words to her are "Wretched queen, adieu!" His time is short. However, he does manage to speak to Horatio several times before he dies.

These few words are short shrift. Hamlet should have done better. The queen was always concerned for him. She grew much closer after Polonius died. The prince remained as distant from her as ever.

Hamlet and Polonius

Aware that Ophelia has been spending a great deal of time with Hamlet, Polonius suspects that his intentions toward her are not honourable. He orders her to stop seeing him immediately. His attitude changes, however, when he believes he has discovered that the prince's madness results from the loss of that relationship. After he and Claudius agree to witness a meeting between Hamlet and Ophelia, Polonius comes upon Hamlet reading a book.

When Polonius asks if the prince recognizes him, Hamlet calls him a fishmonger, Elizabethan slang for the father of a prostitute. Polonius takes the meaning literally, denying that it applies to him. The prince suddenly asks if he has a daughter. When Polonius says he does, Hamlet advises him to take care that she not become pregnant. Polonius thinks Hamlet is speaking dementedly of Ophelia. He takes the prince's words as an indication that the loss of Ophelia has driven him mad.

When Polonius asks about the book Hamlet has been reading, the prince calls it a slanderous work that catalogues the shortcomings of old men. Many of them apply to Polonius, who fails to realize that the prince is having him on. As Polonius takes his leave, Hamlet continues to mock him. When he is out of earshot, the prince calls him a tedious old fool.

***

Hamlet continues to poke fun at Polonius when he tells the prince of the arrival of the travelling players. Hamlet likens him to the Old Testament figure Jephthah, who inadvertently put his daughter's life at stake to ensure a victory in battle. When Polonius complains that a speech by the First Player is too long, Hamlet suggests that Polonius prefers comic songs and dances or ribald tales. After the speech is over, Hamlet instructs Polonius to look after the needs of the players. He cautions them, however, not to mock the old man.

***

During the nunnery scene, Hamlet suddenly asks Ophelia where her father is. When she tells him (falsely) that Polonius is at home, Hamlet says he should stay locked up there so he can play the fool nowhere else. As *The Murder of Gonzago* is about to be performed, Hamlet mocks Polonius's statement that he once played the role of Julius Caesar in a university production. After the performance is ended, Polonius tells the prince that his mother wishes to speak with him immediately. Hamlet points to a cloud, debating which mammal it most resembles—camel, weasel, or whale. The prince refuses again to take Polonius seriously.

***

In the queen's bedchamber, Hamlet's attitude toward Polonius turns nasty. Angry that he has killed the wrong person, Hamlet calls him a "wretched, rash, intruding fool" who meddled once too often. He tells Gertrude he'll "lug the guts" out of the bedroom. Declaring the old man a "foolish prating knave," he hides the body under a staircase.

When Claudius demands to know where the body is, Hamlet says it's providing food for worms.

***

It's difficult to blame Hamlet for making sport of Polonius. The old man is tedious, incompetent, obtuse. He makes a perfect foil for Hamlet's antic disposition. However, he hardly merits the mockery he receives. There are no indications that Polonius meant him harm, yet the prince expresses little remorse over killing him. Hamlet may be displacing aggressive feelings toward Claudius onto someone who posed no threat.

Hamlet and Rosencrantz & Guildenstern

Hamlet's relationship with his former schoolmates goes from barely cordial to deadly. Intent on discovering the cause of Hamlet's apparent lunacy, Rosencrantz and Guildenstern catch the prince by surprise. Hamlet welcomes them warmly enough, but complains that Denmark is a prison. When his friends disagree, Hamlet becomes mistrustful. Forcing them to admit that they were sent for, he tells them their mission is certain to fail.

Hamlet speaks about his bleak moods, which he says he cannot account for. Hoping to raise his spirits, Rosencrantz and Guildenstern mention the arrival of the travelling players. The prince responds positively. About to meet the players, Hamlet welcomes his friends again. He says that his mother and the king are deceived about his madness, which comes and goes like the shifting of winds. The remark seems lost on his friends.

Rosencrantz and Guildenstern report their lack of success to Claudius and Gertrude. They do say that Hamlet's spirits lifted with the arrival of the players. The king is happy to hear that a play is to be performed.

***

Rosencrantz and Guildenstern confront Hamlet on the king's behalf immediately after the performance of *The Murder of Gonzago*. The prince is manic over the apparent confirmation of Claudius's guilt. He keeps interrupting Rosencrantz and Guildenstern as they tell him of the king's great anger and the queen's wish to speak with him in her bedchamber. Hamlet is well aware that they serve the king and are not to be trusted. They readily accept Claudius's order to accompany Hamlet on the voyage to England.

 The prince fully realizes the threat they pose. In his mother's bedchamber he says he regards his former friends as poisonous snakes whose mission is to lead him into harm's way. He is uncooperative when Rosencrantz and Guildenstern try to find Polonius's body. They bring him before the king. Claudius tells them to get Hamlet on the ship and set sail.

After returning to Denmark, Hamlet tells Horatio of his discovery of the warrant for his death, which he rewrote ordering the executions of Rosencrantz and Guildenstern. When Horatio sounds rueful, Hamlet tells him they got what they deserved. When the ambassadors from England arrive to report their deaths, a dying Hamlet expresses regret that he will not have time to hear the news. Evidently it would have pleased him.

***

It is difficult to feel sorry for Rosencrantz and Guildenstern. They were quick to curry favour with Claudius and never really on Hamlet's side. It is questionable, however, that they deserved violent death. There is no evidence they were aware that Hamlet was to be executed in England. The prince's decision to order their deaths is cruel. Again, Hamlet appears to be displacing aggression onto others. He appears to take pride in how cleverly he arranged their demise.

Hamlet and Laertes

About to leave for France, Laertes warns Ophelia against becoming too intimate with Hamlet. Like his father, he suspects that the prince wishes only to have his way with her. His feelings turn to hatred when he learns of his father's death and witnesses Ophelia's demented state. Her death increases his motivation for revenge. He tells the king he would be prepared to cut the prince's throat in church. At Ophelia's funeral, Laertes calls for great misfortune to fall on his head. He and Hamlet struggle in Ophelia's grave, but are soon parted.

As he and Horatio watch Ophelia's funeral procession, the prince refers to Laertes as a "very noble youth." He tells Horatio later that he regrets his behaviour at the gravesite and wishes to make things right with Laertes. When invited to participate in the fencing match, Hamlet says he will honour the queen's request to make amends with Laertes.

When the duel is about to begin, Hamlet's words ring hollow. He blames his wrongdoing on madness that we know to be assumed. The prince says he is as wronged by it as Laertes and assures him the killing of Polonius was unintentional. Laertes accepts the apology conditionally, insisting that a panel of experts on honour rule on its adequacy. He promises meanwhile not to wrong the prince's offer of love.

There is much hypocrisy on both their parts. Laertes mentions a code of honour as he is about to resort to foul play. Hamlet offers an excuse for killing Polonius. Then he predicts that Laertes will outshine him in the match like a bright star in a blackened sky. Laertes accuses Hamlet of mocking him.

***

The match goes in Hamlet's favour. Flushed with success, he accuses Laertes of not making his best efforts. The two men fight fiercely to a draw. As they are resting, Laertes wounds Hamlet with the poisoned sword. In the struggle, Hamlet seizes Laertes' sword, wounding him in return.

Laertes reaches out to Hamlet, taking responsibility for his treachery and implicating the king. He asks Hamlet to exchange forgiveness. The prince's response, "Heaven make thee free of it! I follow thee," sounds dismissive. Hamlet seems in no mood to forgive.

In his relations with Laertes, Hamlet shows little that is admirable. The prince does tell Horatio he regretted his behaviour at Ophelia's grave, but he makes no sincere apology at the fencing match. During the match, we see Hamlet taunt his adversary. As they are about to die, he appears to spurn Laertes' offer of forgiveness. While Hamlet's bitterness is understandable, most of the demeaning treatment of Laertes occurs before and during the match. The prince had been prevailing. He might have been gracious and considerate. He had after all killed Laertes' father. And it is Laertes' blaming of the king that leads to Hamlet's killing Claudius.

III. HAMLET'S SOLILOQUIES

Another method of looking at Hamlet's character is to examine his soliloquies. They are many in number, some quite long. The thoughts and feelings the prince expresses provide insights unavailable elsewhere. They cast more light on how his mind works.

Soliloquy I: Too Too Solid Flesh (i.ii)

Hamlet's first soliloquy follows the promise he gives Claudius and Gertrude to remain in Denmark. He speaks bitterly and in despair. His first thought is to wish his body would simply melt away. He regrets that religion forbids the taking of one's own life. Hamlet finds the current state of the world "weary, stale, flat, and unprofitable." His mood is bleak.

Hamlet is disconsolate over the death of a beloved father and angry about his mother's marriage to Claudius less than two months later. He describes the depth of his father's love for Gertrude and her devotion and dependence upon him. Comparing his father to a sun god and Claudius to a satyr, he blames Gertrude for marrying so soon after Old Hamlet's death. Hamlet regards their union as incestuous, predicting it will come to no good. Heartbroken, he complains of having to keep these feelings to himself. He seems powerless and frustrated.

It is understandable Hamlet would be downcast over the death of his father. The reason for his aversion to Claudius is not yet clear. It may be Hamlet expected to succeed his father as king and regards Claudius as a usurper. His distress over Gertrude's decision to marry Claudius so soon is also understandable.

Soliloquy II: O All You Host Of Heaven (i.iv)

After his meeting with the ghost, Hamlet swears to remember all he has been told. He becomes manic, repeating several times his intention to focus solely on what he has heard. He calls Gertrude a "pernicious woman" and Claudius a "smiling, damnèd villain," but does not speak specifically of taking revenge. When Horatio and Marcellus catch up with him, he says little about the ghost. He soon declares an intention to assume an "antic disposition", and swears his friends to secrecy over what they have seen that night.

Hamlet says the time out of joint and that it is a "cursèd spite" to have to correct it. He appears to be referring to his obligation to avenge his father's murder. His motivation is apparently not strong.

Soliloquy III: Rogue And Peasant Slave (ii.ii)

Inspired by an impassioned speech by the First Player about a character from fiction, Hamlet upbraids himself for the long delay in avenging his father's murder. He attributes his inactivity to cowardice, then lashes out angrily against Claudius. Hamlet accuses himself of expressing what is in his heart in words only, as a whore might. Recovering, it occurs to him to have Claudius witness a play into which he will incorporate the ghost's version of his father's death. Hamlet says that the slightest guilty response by Claudius will provide all the justification he needs to proceed against the king. He thinks the ghost may be a creature of the devil, out to mislead him. Hamlet insists on harder evidence before taking action.

He may be overreaching. If Claudius does react in an apparently guilty manner, Hamlet will have a private confirmation of the ghost's story. However, it would take a confession from the king to justify acting against him. That may or may not happen. If it doesn't, Hamlet will be much worse off. There would be a reprisal from Claudius. The risk is high.

Soliloquy IV: To Be Or Not To Be (iii.i)

Immediately prior to his meeting with Ophelia in the nunnery scene, Hamlet considers whether or not to take his own life. He wonders if it is better to suffer adversity passively or take direct action. He thinks death may be like sleep, therefore an appealing end to worldly difficulties. Second thought leads him to conclude that dread over what may happen after death undercuts the intent to end one's life. We struggle on with the "ills we have" rather than confront what we cannot anticipate. The prince observes that such thinking paralyzes the will, making "cowards of us all." We shrink from undertakings of great importance.

This soliloquy occurs close in time to the previous one, in which Hamlet concluded cowardice was the reason for delaying his revenge. He promised to act against Claudius if he reacts in a guilty manner as he watches the play. Here he offers a rationale that validates cowardice: the uncertain outcome of actions that demand to be undertaken. The prince may be undermining his resolve to kill Claudius even if he does react in a guilty manner.

Soliloquy V: 'Tis Now The Very Witching Time Of Night (iii.ii)

On his way to his mother's bedchamber, Hamlet says that because supernatural creatures abound in the night, his mind is full of murderous thoughts. He seems tempted to act them out against Gertrude, then settles only for a verbal attack. The prince is manic over the apparent success of the play. His bloody thoughts are understandable. He considers directing them however against his mother, who has murdered no one. It's Claudius he needs to kill. His opportunity is about to occur.

Soliloquy VI: Now Might I Do It Pat (iii.iii)

Hamlet encounters Claudius alone and attempting to pray. The prince resolves to kill him on the spot. He stops himself, however, speculating that, because Claudius is at prayer and "purging...his soul," killing him would send him to heaven. Old Hamlet was murdered unshriven of his sins. Hamlet decides to wait until the king's soul would be certain to go to hell. He says killing Claudius now would amount to an assassination.

Hamlet appears ready to shed blood. An instant later, he holds back. His reasoning appears plausible. Ironically, Claudius's attempt at prayer is futile. The king would have died in a sinful state. Considered more deeply, the prince's reasoning seems like an excuse for delay. He might have been more convincing had he mentioned dire consequences for killing Claudius. His justification would have been the king's reaction to a scene from a play. We are seeing once again Hamlet's tendency to undercut almost immediately a declared intention to act.

Soliloquy VII: How All Occasions Do Inform Against Me (iv,iv)

On the way to the ship bound for England, Hamlet learns that the army of Young Fortinbras is marching toward Poland to fight for a "little patch of ground" that is virtually worthless. The prince berates himself again over the long delay in avenging his father's murder. He says God has given man the faculty of reason to use when facing a challenge. He maintains that the cowardly tendency to ruminate over the outcome of an action makes one hesitate to take it. Hamlet declares that he has the justification, willingness, power, and means to proceed against Claudius. He regards the expedition undertaken by Young Fortinbras as one of many examples of attempting to achieve an end involving risk and danger, no matter how insignificant the end might be. The prince says that greatness of mind requires restraint when cause is insufficient, but a compelling necessity to act when honour is involved. Reminding himself that his cause is just, he resolves to cease his shameful delaying. From now on, he maintains, his thoughts will be worthless if they are not bloody.

Although he is about to board a ship, the prince seems ready to act against Claudius. He manages to escape and return to Denmark. He immediately notifies the king by letter that he will visit shortly. Claudius begins to plot against his life. Despite possessing the king's warrant for his death, Hamlet seems in no hurry to confront Claudius. He agrees to take part in a fencing match with Laertes. It is difficult to detect thoughts that are bloody. An intention to act weakens when the opportunity arises.

The sequence of soliloquies follows a repetitive pattern. The prince keeps acknowledging his obligation to avenge his father's murder, but fails to act upon it time and again. It is only when the fencing match ends in disaster that, about to die himself, Hamlet kills Claudius. The only bloody thought he acted on deliberately was his decision to send Rosencrantz and Guildenstern to their deaths.

SUMMATION: HAMLET

The catalogue of shortcomings in Hamlet is not to suggest he is without redeeming qualities. There is the warm bond with Horatio and the relationship with Ophelia as it must have been prior to the ghost's revelations. Hamlet is at his best when he welcomes the travelling players, engages in verbal sparring with the gravedigger, and lampoons Osric when he invites Hamlet to fence with Laertes. The respect Hamlet shows Young Fortinbras also speaks well for him. There is Hamlet's acerbic wit, skill with the sword, and great respect for his father. There is also a tendency to see something of ourselves mirrored in Hamlet that accounts for our fascination with him over the generations.

Nonetheless, the abusive treatment of Ophelia, the disrespect shown Polonius alive and dead, the condescending attitude toward Laertes, the neglect of the queen, and the decision to send Rosencrantz and Guildenstern to their deaths necessitate setting sympathy for Hamlet aside. Avenging his father's murder took too many other lives.

IV. CLAUDIUS AND OTHER CHARACTERS

After looking at Hamlet with a critical eye, we turn to Claudius in search of appealing qualities. We examine his relationships with other characters, the manner in which he conducts himself as king, and the thoughts he expresses in his soliloquies.

Claudius and Rosencrantz & Guildenstern

After Hamlet assumes an antic disposition, Claudius summons to court the prince's long-time friends, Rosencrantz and Guildenstern. He urges them to spend time with the prince to try to discover the cause of his disordered behaviour. Rosencrantz and Guildenstern are happy to cooperate. Gertrude sends them immediately to Hamlet, who greets them warmly enough but tells them their mission cannot succeed. When Rosencrantz and Guildenstern report that Hamlet will reveal nothing, the king appears to be losing patience. He is happy, however, to hear of Hamlet's involvement with the travelling players.

Rosencrantz and Guildenstern begin to serve as royal henchmen. Immediately after the play-within-the-play, they accost Hamlet, telling him of the king's great anger and of the queen's request to speak with him in her bedchamber. Rosencrantz makes a futile attempt to discover the cause of Hamlet's apparent madness. They willingly accept the king's command to accompany Hamlet on the voyage to England.

After the death of Polonius, Claudius sends them to find Hamlet and recover the body of the old man. All they can manage is to bring the prince to the king. When Hamlet runs off, Claudius urges them to follow and get him aboard ship immediately.

Their loyalty to and willingness to serve Claudius speak well for Rosencrantz and Guildenstern. The king has an air about him that inspires allegiance and commands respect. He is confident enough to delegate important duties to trusted subordinates.

Claudius and Polonius

Before granting Laertes' request to return to France, Claudius makes sure that the young man has his father's approval. When Polonius says he has given reluctant consent, Claudius tells Laertes to spend his time as he wishes. Claudius is deferential toward important members of court.

When Polonius says he is convinced that Ophelia's ending her relationship with Hamlet has led to the prince's madness, Claudius asks for proof. Polonius proposes a meeting between Hamlet and Ophelia that he and the king will observe in hiding. Polonius is acting as the prudent and loyal servant of the king. Claudius is cautious and wise, needing stronger evidence. He does not receive it when Hamlet and Ophelia meet in the nunnery scene. The king concludes that Hamlet is more dangerous than insane, and that his objectionable behaviour is not due to the breakup with Ophelia.

Wary of the prince, Claudius considers sending him to England to collect neglected tribute. The king asks Polonius for his opinion. The old man approves but presses with great respect for a second testing of his theory. He suggests that Gertrude question Hamlet in her bedchamber regarding his "griefs," while he hides behind an arras and listens. Claudius agrees, stressing the need to keep Hamlet under careful watch.

Polonius's deviousness costs him his life. The prince runs a sword through the arras, believing that Claudius was behind it. When Gertrude tells Claudius of the old man's death, the king's first thought is that Hamlet could have killed him had he been behind the arras.

Resolving to send the prince immediately to England, Claudius worries over how to acknowledge publicly and explain Polonius's death. He fails to express sympathy or sorrow over his trusted adviser's death.

After Ophelia's mad scene, Claudius speaks to Gertrude of "good Polonius's death." When Laertes returns from France, Claudius says he is "most sensibly in grief" over his father's death and that he loved Polonius. These caring remarks mitigate to some extent Claudius's concern with his own safety and reputation. He is newly established on the throne and Hamlet is very dangerous. When the prince's actions threaten Claudius, his instinct for self-preservation takes over. Feeling more secure, Claudius appears regretful of the old man's death.

At all times Polonius is the king's devoted servant. As with Rosencrantz and Guildenstern, there appears to be a quality in the king's demeanour that inspires loyalty and willing service.

Claudius and Ophelia

Ophelia is present as Polonius and the king are finalizing arrangements to observe the meeting between her and Hamlet. Although some words pass between Ophelia and Gertrude, the king pays her scant attention. When the meeting is over, he says nothing to her.

Claudius attends better when, in a demented state, Ophelia seeks out Gertrude shortly before Laertes returns from France. Distracted over the killing of her father, Ophelia sings portions of a love song that touch tangentially upon Polonius's death. Then she recites an unseemly poem for which the king reproves her. When she departs, Claudius sends Horatio to keep watch over her. In his private remarks to Gertrude shortly after, the king mentions, "poor Ophelia / Divided from herself and her fair judgment." He appears to have genuine concerns about her.

After Laertes confronts the king, Ophelia returns, singing of her father again. When she distributes flowers to those present, Claudius receives fennel, a symbol of flattery. The king is preoccupied with

Laertes and does not speak to Ophelia. As the men plot against Hamlet, Gertrude brings news of Ophelia's death. Laertes withdraws to hide his tears. When Claudius and the queen follow after, he fears that Laertes will become enraged again. He makes no mention of Ophelia.

At Ophelia's funeral, Claudius pays her remains little attention because he needs to intervene in the quarrel between Hamlet and Laertes. He does however promise a fitting marker for her grave. The king's concerns for Ophelia sound sincere. Because his focus has been on Hamlet, he has left it to the queen to attend to Ophelia.

Claudius and Laertes

Relations between Claudius and Laertes are cordial when the king grants him permission to return to France. They are much different when the young man and his followers storm the palace intent on avenging Polonius's death. Claudius calmly faces the young man down. He promises revenge and assures Laertes that he had no part in his father's death. They are interrupted by the brief appearance of Ophelia. Her demented state increases Laertes' motivation for vengeance. Claudius seizes the moment. Together they plan to have Hamlet killed.

Claudius's poise when confronted by Laertes is impressive. When he and the queen are at Laertes' mercy, Claudius plays upon the young man's skill with the sword. Although the plan is treacherous, the king shows boldness, presence of mind, apparent cleverness, and meticulous attention to detail.

At Ophelia's gravesite, Claudius intervenes between Hamlet and Laertes, reminding the young man that his revenge will come soon. During the fencing match, the plot against Hamlet falls apart. After Laertes and Hamlet wound each other with the poisoned sword, Laertes blames the treachery on the king. Hamlet kills Claudius. Gertrude had already drunk the poisoned wine. Claudius and Laertes reap what they have sown.

Claudius and Gertrude

At the council meeting early in the play, Gertrude supports the king's wish that Hamlet cease mourning for his father and remain in Denmark rather than return to university in Wittenberg. Their alliance is evident again when Rosencrantz and Guildenstern try to discover what is troubling Hamlet. The queen promises them a substantial reward if they are successful.

When Polonius says he has found the cause of Hamlet's disordered behaviour, Gertrude agrees that it could be due to the loss of his relationship with Ophelia. Claudius suspects more troubling reasons. They decide to test Polonius's theory. Just before Ophelia and Hamlet meet, the queen hopes that the loss of Ophelia's "good beauties" does account for Hamlet's misbehaviour. Claudius remains wary and suspicious. Events in the nunnery scene increase his concerns. The alliance between king and queen over how to deal with Hamlet appears to weaken.

During the preliminaries to the play-within-the-play, Hamlet declines his mother's request to sit by her. Claudius and Gertrude become uneasy as the Player Queen swears never to remarry. Gertrude finds her remarks excessive. Claudius asks Hamlet if the play contains any offence. He is greatly startled when poison is poured into the ear of the sleeping Player King. The king becomes angry and resolves to send Hamlet immediately to England. The queen summons Hamlet to her bedchamber to discipline him. Claudius and Gertrude appear to be drawing close again.

Events in the closet scene greatly affect the relationship between Claudius and Gertrude. She repents of her adultery and promises not to reveal that Hamlet is not insane. The change is evident immediately. When Gertrude tells Claudius that Hamlet has killed Polonius, she blames his madness and says that he weeps over what he has done. The queen is protective of her son and deliberately misleading Claudius. The king tells her that Hamlet must leave for England at sunrise.

During Ophelia's mad scene, both Claudius and Gertrude are distressed at her mental state. When Laertes confronts Claudius after returning from France, Gertrude becomes indignant and tries to protect the king. Claudius tells her not to be afraid and appeases Laertes. Gertrude interrupts Claudius and Laertes' plotting to report Ophelia's death. The queen's role in this sequence is largely passive. Claudius is absorbed in the plan to kill Hamlet.

At the funeral of Ophelia, Gertrude bids her a touching farewell and strews flowers on her grave. When Hamlet clashes with Laertes, the king orders them separated. He and the queen tell Laertes that Hamlet's madness is to blame. Gertrude is protecting Hamlet. Claudius is trying to calm Laertes. When Hamlet stalks away, the king sends Horatio after him. Addressing her as "good Gertrude," he directs the queen to order a watch kept over Hamlet. Gertrude is very much on Hamlet's side. She does not speak with Claudius anywhere in this scene.

Gertrude is distant from the king throughout the duel scene. During a break in the fighting, she offers Hamlet her handkerchief to wipe perspiration from his brow. To toast Hamlet's success in the match, the queen reaches for the cup containing the poisoned wine. Over Claudius's objection, she insists on drinking, seemingly defying him. When the fight resumes, Gertrude collapses. With her dying breath, she warns Hamlet not to drink. Claudius insists that she has only fainted.

Few words pass between king and queen in this scene. Claudius is dealing with the unravelling of the plan to have Hamlet killed. The denial of the queen's death indicates the depth of the feelings he still has for her. Gertrude has been focused exclusively on Hamlet. When she warns him not to drink, her alliance with him is stronger than ever. She is completely distant from the king.

Gertrude moves progressively from a strong alliance with Claudius to a strengthening attachment to Hamlet. The king is deeply committed to her throughout the play. His care becomes stronger after the closet scene. He appeals for her support in making the news of Polonius's death public. After the mad scene, he mentions all the sorrows they face. Claudius tells Laertes how "conjunctive to [his] life and soul" Gertrude has been. He refers to her as "sweet queen" and "good Gertrude." He tries to stop her from drinking the poisoned wine and is in denial over her death.

Claudius's love for Gertrude is deep and true. That speaks well for him. Although it hardly begins to mitigate the evil he has done, it reveals a human side to his character. The king is not absolutely bad.

Claudius as Monarch

Newly established on the throne, Claudius holds what appears to be his first council meeting. He thanks the assembled courtiers for accepting his hasty marriage to Gertrude and participating in the mourning for Old Hamlet. To cope with the threat posed by Young Fortinbras, Claudius sends Cornelius and Voltimand with letters for Old Norway, asking that he rein his nephew in. After Claudius attends to Laertes and Hamlet, proceedings are adjourned. Except for the prince, the company withdraws to celebrate with drinks and cannon fire.

The appeal to Old Norway soon bears fruit. Cornelius and Voltimand return with news that Old Norway has reprimanded his nephew for intending to invade Denmark and directed him to attack Poland instead. At this point in his reign, Claudius appears every inch a king. He acquits himself well with internal matters and affairs of state.

The king is soon forced to deal with his troublesome nephew. Claudius acts quickly, summoning Rosencrantz and Guildenstern to court. He uses them to try to discover what is troubling Hamlet. Claudius employs others to act on his behalf: Voltimand and Cornelius, Polonius, and his vassals in England. This is appropriate behaviour on the part of the king. He does not hesitate to assign duties to persons he trusts.

Claudius acts swiftly after the nunnery scene. He rejects the forbidden love theory, expresses doubt that Hamlet is mad, and considers sending the prince on state business. Agreeing to a second testing of Polonius's theory, he mentions the need to keep a wary eye on Hamlet. The king is shrewd and able to make decisions quickly. The second testing occurs that very evening. Claudius is functioning effectively.

At *The Murder of Gonzago*, Claudius learns that Hamlet somehow knows the cause of his father's death. After a momentary panic, he decides to send him immediately to England. He recovers quickly from an adverse situation, which becomes more urgent with the death of Polonius. The king instructs his vassals in England to execute the prince the moment he arrives. Claudius is capable of ruthlessness in order to maintain his hold on the crown. His instinct for self-preservation is a characteristic of effective rulers. He does not hesitate to do what needs to be done.

When Laertes returns from France with armed supporters, Claudius says the divinity that hedges kings will protect him. He hears Laertes out and assures him that he had no part in Polonius's death. He persuades the young man to join him in plotting Hamlet's death. Claudius shows considerable physical courage. His life and the queen's are at risk, yet Claudius remains calm and unafraid. These are attributes becoming in a king.

At Ophelia's funeral he ends the struggle between Hamlet and Laertes. He tells Gertrude to keep watch over Hamlet, promises a fitting marker for Ophelia's grave, and leads the procession away for an hour of reflection. Although Hamlet's appearance was unexpected, Claudius manages the situation well enough.

The king presides over the fencing match between Hamlet and Laertes. Before it begins, he attempts to make peace between the two men. Claudius has Osric provide the foils and makes sure Hamlet understands the wagering. The king orders the kettledrum struck, the trumpet sounded, and cannons fired. He instructs the judges to observe the action closely.

Once the duel begins, Claudius loses control. Gertrude drinks the poisoned wine. Laertes and Hamlet wound each other fatally. When Laertes blames the king for the foul play, Hamlet kills Claudius, bids the queen farewell, then dies himself. As Laertes is dying, he says the king is "justly serv'd." It is hard to disagree. Since the play-within-the-play, Claudius resorted to desperate measures that proved very costly.

To his credit, Claudius did experience a lash of conscience as he and Polonius prepared for the meeting of Ophelia and Hamlet. In soliloquy after the play-within-the-play, the king considers repentance for his brother's murder. Unwilling to give up its rewards, he casts moral considerations aside. He does whatever is necessary to maintain his hold on queen and crown.

Despite showing much that is becoming in a king, Claudius remains an adulterous murderer. Although he gained the throne unjustly, it is tempting to think about how good a king he might have made under legitimate circumstances.

V. CLAUDIUS'S SOLILOQUIES

As with Hamlet, we examine Claudius's soliloquies in detail. Few in number, they do provide insights not fully apparent elsewhere.

Soliloquy I: O! 'Tis Too True (iii.i)

This lengthy aside occurs as Claudius hears Polonius instructing Ophelia to appear to be reading a holy book when she confronts Hamlet in the nunnery scene. Polonius's observation that it is blameworthy to mask shameful actions with "devotion's image," triggers a pang of remorse in the king. He reminds himself how his evil deeds are covered over by fair-seeming words, as a harlot's true nature can be obscured with makeup.

Despite his serious crimes, Claudius is to a degree a man of conscience. He says his misdeeds impose a "heavy burden." These thoughts have little lasting effect however. Hamlet's abuse of Ophelia causes Claudius to doubt that the prince is insane. Realizing that Hamlet poses a considerable threat, the king considers sending him on a voyage to England. Moral considerations give way to the need to act.

Soliloquy II: O! My Offence Is Rank (iii.iii)

After Polonius leaves to witness Hamlet's meeting with his mother, Claudius considers resorting to prayer to ease his conscience. He admits that the killing of a brother is the most serious of all crimes. His strong feelings of guilt interfere with his intention to pray. Claudius believes that heavenly grace must exist to forgive and pardon, or else mercy would serve no purpose. He says that prayer performs a two-fold function. It can prevent a contemplated act of evil or forgive one already committed. He resolves to try to pray.

The king soon realizes that he cannot seek divine forgiveness while possessing what he murdered for. He says that although in this world the rich and powerful can circumvent justice, it is not so in heaven. There he would need to account for his sins.

Claudius considers repenting but quickly concludes that he cannot because he is unwilling to give up the benefits the murder brought him. He says his soul, struggling to be free of sin, remains focused on the things of this world. He decides to seek help from the angels. Kneeling in momentary prayer, he soon rises because the words sent heavenward belie his thoughts, which are fixed on earth. The attempt at prayer fails.

Again it is clear that Claudius is not lacking in conscience. He acknowledges his guilt and speaks of a wish to atone for it. He hopes that divine intervention will help. The king recognizes, however, that absolution demands sincere repentance, which is simply out of the question. He sets guilt aside in favour of the rewards his crime has brought him. His pattern of thought is coherent. He has made his choice and will act accordingly.

Soliloquy III: And, England, If Thou My Love Hold'st At Aught (iv.iii)

After telling Hamlet he must leave for England for his safety, Claudius orders Rosencrantz and Guildenstern to accompany him. He speaks in soliloquy of letters ordering his vassals there to execute Hamlet on arrival. The king says the prince is a fever in his blood that must be purged before he can be happy again.

The killing of Polonius has greatly shaken Claudius. He fears for his own life but can hardly proceed legally against the prince, who is his wife's son and is regarded highly by the Danish people. The king needs to be protected. Getting Hamlet aboard ship is the first step. Previous indications of conscience do not recur.

The soliloquies show evidence of conscience in Claudius and an inclination to be forgiven for his sins. Weighing his wants and needs against the costs of repentance, he takes action. Despite increasing adversity he stays the course once a decision is made.

SUMMATION: CLAUDIUS

The considerable strengths of the king notwithstanding, he remains deceitful and treacherous. Despite occasional words of remorse, Claudius sets conscience aside as he struggles to hold on to his throne. Before Hamlet meets the ghost, he performs effectively as king. After the play-within-the-play, he manages under increasing duress to continue functioning. Matters eventually spin out of control.

To his credit, Claudius shows concern over Polonius's death and for the madness and death of Ophelia. The extent of his love for Gertrude speaks well for him. He shows strength of purpose, cleverness, insight into self, decisiveness, and willingness to take bold action. Much of the time they serve evil ends. The bad in him far outweighs the good.

CONCLUSIONS

All things considered, neither of these formidable adversaries proved mighty enough. Because no case could be made to justify it, Claudius is unable to take direct action against Hamlet. A strong case, however, might have been made over the killing of Polonius. The plot to have the prince die in the duel with Laertes proved disastrous.

Hamlet never does confront Claudius over the death of his father. The play-within-the-play did that indirectly. The antic disposition allowed Hamlet to act passive-aggressively against less threatening targets. Laertes' denunciation of the king frees Hamlet to avenge his father's death, but the cost in other lives was very high. Defects in character proved the undoing of the mighty opposites. Claudius is overly egocentric and deficient in conscience. Hamlet is mean-spirited and lacking will power.

Defying Augury
God, Fate, Free Will, and Chance in Hamlet

hen he tells Horatio of events on the ship bound for England, Hamlet speaks glowingly of rash actions, which he says "sometimes serve us well" when careful plotting would fail. He mentions his impulsive decision to steal into Rosencrantz and Guildenstern's cabin, where he discovered the grand commission ordering his death. He says such occurrences confirm that our actions are subject to divine oversight, which ensures success no matter how badly they are mismanaged.

The prince is taking a curious position on the free will/determinism issue philosophers have struggled with over the centuries. He suggests that actions taken upon impulse—acts of volition nonetheless—sometimes of themselves accomplish our ends, but whenever they do not, they are subject to remediation through the grace of God. Hamlet seems to believe that impulsive acts can ultimately never go wrong.

After agreeing to fight the duel with Laertes, Hamlet speaks to Horatio again, insisting that the "special providence" governing the fall of a sparrow will influence how the match unfolds. He stresses the need to be prepared for whatever happens, even an early death. The prince is becoming fatalistic. He maintains that what will be will be, and must be accepted. Hamlet appears to believe that outcomes are predetermined.

i

It is understandable that acting on impulse would appeal to Hamlet. In his soliloquies, he mentions more than once that ruminating on the outcome of an action can undermine the motivation to perform it. The prince's trust in the intervention of providence when matters go awry is less understandable. When we recall occasions on which Hamlet acted on impulse, the reason becomes apparent. That behaviour creates more problems than it solves.

Hamlet's first rash decision occurs when, against the advice of Horatio and Marcellus, he insists on following after his father's ghost. He threatens bodily harm if they attempt to restrain him. The benefit of the encounter is that Hamlet hears an account of how his father died, which he accepts as accurate. He promises to remember forever the "commandment" the ghost has given him. However, he quickly loses motivation to act upon it. After swearing Horatio and Marcellus to secrecy, Hamlet calls his obligation to avenge his father's death a "cursèd spite."

At that same time the prince suddenly reveals an intention to act as if he were insane. Although he does not say why, it does allow him to displace aggressive feelings toward Claudius onto less threatening characters, such as Polonius and Ophelia. In any case, episodes of deranged behaviour cause the king to speak to Rosencrantz and Guildenstern about Hamlet's "dangerous and turbulent lunacy." After witnessing the meeting of Hamlet and Ophelia, however, Claudius declares the prince's ranting sane enough. Sensing potential danger, he considers sending him to England on state business. The apparent insanity convinces the king that Hamlet poses a serious threat. Acting insane has made Claudius wary of him.

In soliloquy, Hamlet decides on the spur of the moment to try to induce Claudius to confess his crime by seeing a play in which poison is poured into the ear of a sleeping king. At that point, Claudius calls for light and suddenly withdraws. There is no confession and the king is fully aware of how dangerous Hamlet is. Staging the play has hardly advanced the prince's cause. Claudius orders Rosencrantz and Guildenstern to escort Hamlet on the voyage to England.

Hamlet's situation worsens with the impulsive killing of Polonius. Claudius instructs his vassals in England to execute the prince when he arrives. Hamlet's escape onto the pirate ship thwarts that plan. Back in Denmark, however, he sends Claudius a letter announcing his return. The impulse to jump ship that saved his life is immediately undermined. Claudius and Laertes plot his death.

Laertes' excessive words of mourning at Ophelia's funeral prompt Hamlet to emerge from hiding and jump into her grave. He rants about which of them loved Ophelia more. Claudius restrains Laertes, pointing out that their plot can go forward now that Hamlet is back. Hamlet's rash decision to leap into the grave will shortly lead to a fencing match intended to end his life.

Hamlet's willingness to participate in the match seems impulsive. He hesitates momentarily, but refuses Horatio's offer to beg off. When selecting foils, the prince seems careless, asking only if they are all the same length. After winning the first two bouts, he accuses Laertes rashly of not making his best effort. During a pause in the third bout, an angry Laertes wounds Hamlet with the poisoned sword when he is off guard.

Impulsive behaviour on shipboard did save Hamlet from execution. Following after the ghost did lead to learning the details of his father's death. Much more often, however, acting on impulse did not serve him well. The divinity that shapes our ends was evidently not on his side.

ii

Approaching a churchyard, Hamlet and Horatio come upon a gravedigger who sings as he disturbs the remains of the previously buried. The prince reflects on how people of great importance in life become dust and scattered bones. It causes his own bones to ache when he sees bones being knocked about by the gravedigger's spade. Hamlet comments on the impermanence and perhaps the absurdity of life. When he consents later on to fight the duel with Laertes, his mood lightens. He takes comfort in the providence involved in the fall of a sparrow.

It should come as no surprise to see the prince looking for comfort from divine sources. The play is replete with Hamlet's references to the Christian God and to Christian teachings and beliefs. In his first soliloquy, he refers to the Everlasting's strictures against self-slaughter and cries out to God about how "weary, stale, flat, and unprofitable" he finds the uses of this world. When Horatio tells the prince of his sighting of the ghost, Hamlet's response is, "For God's love let me hear." When first encountering the ghost, Hamlet calls upon "angels and ministers of grace" to defend him. As Horatio and Marcellus try to prevent him from following after it, the prince says that his soul is as immortal as the ghost itself. Hamlet cries, "O God!" when the ghost appears to question how much he loved his father. As it departs, Hamlet swears by all the hosts of heaven, earth, and even hell that its words will never be forgotten. When Horatio asks about what the ghost has said, Hamlet is evasive. He tells his friend that he will retire to pray.

Before welcoming the travelling players, Hamlet likens Polonius to the Old Testament figure Jephthah. During the nunnery scene, the prince complains to Ophelia about how women use makeup to paint over the face that God has given them, and how they apply indecent names to God's creatures. Instructing the First Player on what to avoid during the performance, Hamlet condemns players who lack the attributes of Christians, pagans, or man in general as they shout while performing.

On his way to his mother's bedchamber, the prince decides against killing Claudius at prayer because he believes it would send his soul straight to heaven. Hamlet tells Gertrude that heaven looks with great sorrow on her sin of marrying Claudius. When the ghost intervenes, Hamlet calls for help from heavenly guards. After it has gone, the prince urges his mother to confess to heaven, avoid further sinning with Claudius, and exorcise the devil. Regarding the killing of Polonius, he says, "Heaven has pleased it so, to punish me with this."

Hamlet is steeped in Christian tradition. Speaking to Horatio about divinity and providence, he expresses a belief that God has a plan for us that includes intervention whenever we falter. Hamlet regards the plan as preordained. He stresses the need to be prepared for and accept whatever happens. What does happen seems less than providential. Polonius and Ophelia are already dead. Hamlet is wounded with the envenomed sword, with which he wounds Laertes. Gertrude drinks the poisoned wine. Hamlet kills Claudius after Laertes implicates the king. The murder of Old Hamlet is finally avenged. Dismayed at the sight of all the corpses, Young Fortinbras lays claim to the Danish throne. These occurrences are hardly divinity shaping rough-hewn ends. They are more like the wrath of God descending on a multitude of sinners.

iii

Although he lays heavy emphasis on the Christian God, Hamlet refers on a number of occasions to the goddess Fortune and her involvement in human affairs. Fortune is the early Christian version of the Roman goddess Fortuna. Sometimes regarded as the daughter of Jupiter, she occupied a prominent place in Roman religion. Fortuna was known for her wheel, which became associated with changes in life between prosperity and disaster, often imposed in a capricious and fickle manner. She was influential and controversial in early Christianity for the spinning of her wheel, raising the mighty to power only to bring them crashing down. This wheel became a powerful symbol in the Middle Ages. Medieval images of Fortune often showed her blindfolded, as if blinded to justice. Occasionally, she appeared in provocative dress, affecting the demeanour of a prostitute.

Perhaps it is this aspect that prompts Hamlet to refer to Fortune disparagingly when first meeting Rosencrantz and Guildenstern.

When they tell him that they dwell neither on Fortune's cap nor on the soles of her shoe, Hamlet says they must be dwelling about her waist, in the middle of her favours. When Guildenstern says they are her "privates," the prince mentions her secret parts and calls her a strumpet.

The Trojan hero Aeneas also calls her a strumpet in a speech Hamlet tells us he "chiefly loved." The First Player recites lines in which Aeneas rails against Fortune for permitting Pyrrhus to strike the head of king Priam with his sword. He urges the other gods to destroy her wheel, sending the hub rolling down to Hades. As Hecuba laments Pyrrhus's hacking at her husband's remains, Aeneas says that any witness to the slaughter would have cried out venomously at Fortune for allowing it to happen. He says heaven itself would have wept to hear the clamour of Hecuba's wailing.

These references to the goddess are hardly complimentary. Hamlet's attitude toward fortune as chance, accident, or ill luck is negative throughout the play. On their way to watch for a possible appearance of his father's ghost, Hamlet tells Horatio that the Danish reputation for heavy drinking could be the result of "fortune's star," by which he means bad luck. In a soliloquy, he mentions the "slings and arrows of outrageous fortune." When conferring with Horatio before the play-within-the-play, Hamlet speaks of "fortune's buffets and rewards." He says his friend's constitution will never be a "pipe for fortune's fingers / To sound what stop she please."

During *The Murder of Gonzago*, the Player King questions his wife's assurances that she will never seek a second husband. He respects her good intentions but observes that because it is uncertain whether "love lead fortune or else fortune love," it is quite possible that love "should with our fortunes change." He predicts that her intention never to remarry will die as soon as he does. Again, fortune is being characterized negatively.

Animated by the apparent success of the play-within-the-play, Hamlet remarks that should his own "fortunes ever turn Turk," he could always get work in a theatrical company. After he kills Polonius, Hamlet tells the corpse "take thy fortune" as if the death were unlucky. Proceeding toward the ship bound for England, Hamlet learns that the Norwegian army is out to conquer a virtually worthless part of Poland. In soliloquy, he states that Young Fortinbras and his men are risking "all that fortune, death, and danger dare" for nothing more valuable than an egg shell. In each case, Hamlet appears to associate fortune with negative outcomes.

Although Hamlet does mention fortune's rewards when he speaks to Horatio, he refers to her buffets and her tendency to be arbitrary. All other references stress her malign and capricious nature. The soliloquy involving Young Fortinbras contains Hamlet's final reference to fortune. He puts faith thereafter in a divinity that will reshape rough-hewn ends. He makes no further mention of fickle fortune conspiring against him. It might be that God intended more deaths to occur. The disrespect Hamlet has shown the goddess Fortune may also have been a factor.

iv

Over the course of the play, Hamlet refers occasionally to chance. When telling Horatio of the Danish reputation for excessive drinking, he compares it to a defect that often "chances" in men who otherwise would be held in high regard. He asks Rosencrantz and Guildenstern how it "chances" that the actors have left their theatre in the city to go on the road. He refers to all the deaths in the final scene as "this chance." In each case, Hamlet uses the term in the sense of how an event or situation happened to occur, something in need of explanation. He does not speak of them as something unintentional, a coincidence, or a random occurrence. However, many such events affect him.

The travelling players arrive by chance. The prince decides to stage an amended version of *The Murder of Gonzago*, in which a part of the ghost's version of the murder of Old Hamlet is enacted. The performance fails, however, to produce a confession. Instead, it motivates Claudius to send Hamlet to be executed in England.

The prince used this chance occurrence to try to confirm the ghost's story. Although it does so for himself and Horatio, it lets the king know that Hamlet is on to him. Hamlet promised himself that if Claudius "but blench" during the performance, he would act against the king. Instead, he agrees to undertake the voyage to England. Hamlet substantiated the ghost's story, but left the king with the upper hand. The subsequent slaying of Polonius made matters worse. Hamlet's attempt to turn a chance occurrence to his advantage fails, leaving him in a weakened position.

On the way to his mother's bedchamber, Hamlet happens upon Claudius attempting to pray. The king is preoccupied and defenceless. Hamlet has an unlooked for opportunity to avenge his father's death. He forbears because he fears he would be sending Claudius's soul to heaven. The king's attempt at prayer fails. His soul would have gone to perdition. Hamlet could have acted when he had the king at his mercy.

On the way to the ship bound for England, Hamlet meets by chance the forces of Young Fortinbras. The prince is impressed with Fortinbras's willingness to take considerable risk for a patch of ground that is virtually worthless. Hamlet says he will use the occasion to turn his thoughts bloody. They become actions only when he orders the deaths of Rosencrantz and Guildenstern. When the fencing match goes awry, Hamlet does manage to kill Claudius when everything else is lost.

As they plot Hamlet's death, Claudius tells Laertes that when Hamlet heard a visitor from France praise Laertes' skill with the sword, the prince could hardly wait to challenge him to a fencing match. This visit allows Claudius to use the match, which Hamlet would hardly refuse, as a means of having him die as if by accident. The prince is about to be victimized as the result a random occurrence.

Regarding the voyage to England, Hamlet tells Horatio that heavenly ordinance was responsible for his father's signet being in his purse. The prince used it to seal the writ for the deaths of Rosencrantz and Guildenstern. Possession of the signet might be regarded more realistically as a coincidence that helped him order the deaths of his former friends. Although this action does him little credit, having the signet made the order official.

In a letter to Horatio, Hamlet mentions the pirates' attack on the ship bound for England. This coincidence allows the prince to return to Denmark with documentary evidence that might justify killing the king. Instead, Hamlet sends a letter to Claudius announcing his return and an intention to visit him the next day. The decision to forewarn Claudius is puzzling. Why not arrive unannounced, using the order for his death as justification for the killing the king? Claudius and Laertes now plot the prince's death. Once again, Hamlet passes up an opportunity to avenge his father's murder.

Accompanied by Horatio, Hamlet comes by chance upon the funeral rites for Ophelia. He confronts Laertes over his excessive words of mourning. When Claudius intervenes, Hamlet stalks away. The king tells Laertes that vengeance will come soon. Chancing upon Ophelia's funeral puts the prince's life in serious jeopardy.

When Laertes wounds Hamlet with the poisoned sword tip, the two accidentally pick up the other's weapon in the struggle that ensues. Hamlet wounds Laertes, who blames Claudius for the foul play. The prince is finally able to avenge his father's murder. Had chance not led to the exchange of swords, Laertes and Claudius would have lived on, and the murder of Old Hamlet would not have been avenged.

***

The arrival of the traveling players provided Hamlet with a strong indication of Claudius's guilt. Meeting the army of Young Fortinbras gave him fleeting inspiration for proceeding against the king. The encounter with the pirate ship allowed him to return to Denmark with hard evidence against Claudius. The exchange of swords led to the killing of the king.

Refraining from killing Claudius at prayer was an opportunity lost. Killing Polonius in his mother's bedchamber put Hamlet in harm's way. Interrupting the funeral service permitted Claudius to lure Hamlet into the fencing match.

Hamlet's reluctance to take advantage of situations created by chance led to his downfall. Had he acted more resolutely, he would have avenged his father's murder at the possible cost of only his own life. The prince appears incapable of seizing the day. He seems to prefer engaging in gratuitous acts: lampooning Polonius, haranguing Ophelia, excoriating Gertrude, and sending Rosencrantz and Guildenstern to their deaths.

***

Hamlet's praise of rash actions and his conviction that there is a divinity that shapes our ends occur immediately after the deplorable episode at Ophelia's grave. His mention of the special providence involved in the fall of a sparrow comes after he has agreed to fence with Laertes. By that time, many of his impulsive acts have left him at considerable disadvantage. Claudius had already tried to have him killed. The death of Polonius has Laertes thirsting for revenge. Yet Hamlet appears to have no urgent need to proceed against the king. He seems content to fight the duel and let God's plan unfold as it will.

With the duel about to begin, however, he becomes more active. In the apology he offers Laertes over killing Polonius, he blames his madness, although moments after the old man's death, he told Gertrude that he is only "mad in craft." When selecting foils, Laertes accuses Hamlet of mocking him. During a period of rest, Hamlet accuses Laertes of not making his best efforts. When it is clear that both will die, Hamlet appears to dismiss Laertes' request to exchange forgiveness. The prince's behaviour during the duel scene is impulsive and unkind.

As on many other occasions, Hamlet's impulsive actions here do not serve him well. Nor does it appear here or at other times that divinity was at work shaping rough-hewn ends. Any part the goddess Fortune may have been playing was more a buffet than a reward, perhaps because of the disrespect Hamlet showed her. The prince's failure to turn chance occurrences to full advantage led to his death. Although he avenged his father's murder, too many other lives were lost as well.

Frailty, is Woman thy True Name?

Ⅎn his first soliloquy, Hamlet is deeply troubled by his mother's decision to marry Claudius, whom he despises, so soon after Old Hamlet's death. He reacts by condemning women in general. "Frailty, thy name is woman!" he declares, unhappy that he must keep these bitter feelings to himself. Since Hamlet does not yet know of Gertrude's adultery with Claudius or of his uncle's murder of Old Hamlet, the statement seems excessive. There might be reason to believe that Gertrude is frail, but that hardly justifies making frailty the defining characteristic of womankind. The remark does invite, however, an assessment of the strength of character displayed by each of the women in the play.

i

About to depart for France, Laertes lectures Ophelia about the dangers of allowing Hamlet to have his way with her. She promises to keep in her heart all he has said, but does not indicate that it will govern her behaviour. Instead, she cautions him to be sure to follow his own advice. After Laertes leaves, Polonius confronts Ophelia over the amount of time she has been spending with Hamlet. When she insists that the prince has made declarations of love in "honourable fashion," Polonius tells her not to believe them and that Hamlet is beguiling her. He orders her to have no further communication with him. Ophelia promises to obey.

Ophelia's report of Hamlet's disturbing visit to her sewing room convinces Polonius that the prince is mad for her love. When he asks if Ophelia had spoken harshly to Hamlet, she says she sent his letters back and refused to see him. Blaming himself for mistaking Hamlet's motives, he tells Ophelia to come with him to report everything to the king.

In her dealings with her father, Ophelia shows an appropriate assertiveness regarding Hamlet's intentions, but a willingness to sever that relationship when ordered to. She reacts with a more light-hearted assertiveness when her brother warns her against Hamlet. These are appealing qualities. Ophelia is an agreeable sister and a dutiful daughter who is apparently still in love with Hamlet.

***

Matters do not go well for Ophelia in the nunnery scene. She and Hamlet meet as if by accident. Ophelia offers him love tokens she had been intending to return for some time. When he denies having given her anything, she becomes irritated, insisting that he knows full well that he did. She says the gifts were accompanied by words of love that made them more valuable. Their value fallen, she urges him to take them back.

Hamlet asks if she is both chaste ("honest" is the word he uses) and beautiful. When he insists that beauty and chastity do not go hand in hand because beautiful women are seldom chaste, Ophelia replies that beauty could want no better relationship than with chastity. Hamlet appears to be calling her chastity into question while she defends it.

Admitting that he once did love her, he immediately denies it. Ophelia says she believed him but realizes now that she was being deceived. Urging her to live in a nunnery, Hamlet declares all men knaves and all women wanton. As he rants on, Ophelia calls upon heavenly powers to help him. When he has gone, she expresses sorrow over his mental state and its devastating effects on their relationship.

The returning of the love tokens may have been intended to elicit words of love from the prince. Hamlet's reaction is a tirade that creates feelings of sorrow and regret in Ophelia. She tries to stand her ground, but his ranting renders her almost speechless. Polonius and the king have put her in a difficult situation. She is trying to please them by confronting Hamlet. Apparently unhappy over the breakup of their relationship, the prince treats her harshly. The attempt to validate the forbidden love theory does not succeed. Ophelia is forthright with Hamlet at first. After he has gone, her lament over what his madness has done to their relationship indicates that she still cares for him.

***

During the preliminaries to *The Murder of Gonzago*, Hamlet declines his mother's invitation to sit by her, declaring Ophelia "metal more attractive." The prince lies at Ophelia's feet, asking if he may lie in her lap. When she refuses, he says he meant with his head upon her lap, to which she consents. Hamlet asks if she thought he meant "country matters." Ophelia says she thinks nothing, as if to pre-empt further talk. The prince mentions how fair a thought it is to "lie between maids' legs." Her reply, "What is, my lord?" is likely uttered in a tone of disapproval. For the moment, Hamlet ceases his unseemly remarks.

After the presentation of the dumb-show, Ophelia seems puzzled. When the speaker of the prologue appears, she asks if he will clarify its meaning. Hamlet says the Prologue will comment on anything she wishes to show him. He urges her not to be ashamed of the showing because the Prologue will have no shame in telling her what it means. Ophelia says that because he is disgusting, she will concentrate on the play.

When the dialogue between the Player King and Queen is over, Ophelia praises Hamlet's skill in interpreting the play. He replies that he would interpret between her and her lover if he could "see the puppets dallying." To her comment that his wit is keen, the prince tells her it would cost her "a groaning to take off [his] edge." Hamlet uses his nearness to Ophelia to badger her with lewd remarks. She does assert herself, however, when he goes too far.

***

Following the death of Polonius, a distraught Ophelia seeks out the queen, who at first is reluctant to see her. Ophelia sings of the death of a true love who died unmourned. Claudius associates the song with her father's death. When Ophelia breaks into a bawdy song, the king reproves her. Before leaving, she speaks of Polonius's death, indicating that Laertes will hear of it.

Ophelia reappears when Claudius is consoling Laertes over his father's death. Laertes is overcome at her mental state. Ophelia begins to sing of her father's funeral and distributes various flowers to those present. Sorrowful over his death, she sings another song of mourning.

As Claudius and Laertes plot against Hamlet, the queen interrupts to report Ophelia's death. Gertrude tells them that covered with flowers, she fell into a brook from a broken branch in a willow tree, singing until her waterlogged clothing caused her to drown. At her funeral Laertes' argument with the priest and Hamlet's rant over the extent of his love for her profaned what should have been a dignified ceremony.

***

Prior to Polonius's death, it is difficult to detect much frailty in Ophelia. She appeared self-possessed and strong-willed, able to engage lovingly with her brother and respectfully with her father. Despite Hamlet's abusive behaviour in her sewing room and during the nunnery scene, Ophelia expressed admiration for him and sorrow over what his madness had done to their relationship. At *The Murder of Gonzago*, she kept the prince at arm's length, deflecting his provocative remarks.

Ophelia's sanity broke down over her father's death at the hands of the man she had loved. She was suffering a severe loss. Despite the priest's insistence that Ophelia's death was a suicide, she was clearly not in her right mind. Her apparent failure to try to save herself could hardly be considered intentional.

ii

Gertrude's overly quick marriage to Claudius and insufficient mourning of the death of Old Hamlet caused Hamlet much pain. He regards her as weak-willed and immoral. When he learns from his father's ghost of her adultery with Claudius, the prince calls his mother "pernicious," as if she were wicked or evil. Because the ghost forbade him from acting against Gertrude, Hamlet's contact with his mother prior to their meeting after the play-within-the-play is minimal. Once Claudius's guilt is confirmed, Hamlet harangues her over her blindness in preferring Claudius to his father, to the point where the ghost intervenes on Gertrude's behalf. Hamlet orders his mother to become emotionally distant from the king and not reveal that his madness is assumed.

While Gertrude has certainly sinned, she does begin to show remorse. In the closet scene, she says that his words are like daggers in her ears. Hamlet relents, urging Gertrude to confess to heaven and be repentant. The queen is won over. She promises to reveal nothing to Claudius about what has passed between them that night, and appears distressed when Hamlet speaks of the upcoming voyage to England.

When she tells Claudius of Polonius's death, she misleads him by attributing the killing to Hamlet's insanity and says that he weeps over what he has done. Before meeting the grieving Ophelia, Gertrude speaks in an aside of her sin-sick soul and anticipates dire consequences.

After trying to protect Claudius when Laertes confronts him over Polonius's death, Gertrude becomes progressively distant from the king. She does not respond when he mentions all the sorrows they are facing, and plays no part when Claudius and Laertes plot the death of Hamlet. At Ophelia's funeral, she expresses hope that Hamlet and Ophelia would have wed, and makes excuses for her son when he clashes with Laertes. During the fencing match, she offers to wipe Hamlet's brow and disobeys Claudius when he tries to stop her from drinking to Hamlet's success from the poisoned cup. With her dying breath, Gertrude warns her son not to drink.

Although Gertrude's attempts to atone for her sins prove unavailing, it was not for lack of trying. Her willingness to atone showed strength of character despite the weakness apparent in her adultery with Claudius. There was little else she could have done. Hamlet's fate was sealed when he killed Polonius.

Hamlet's confrontational behaviour in the closet scene brings Gertrude face to face with her sinfulness and gets her fully on his side. There are also previous indications of genuine concern for him. She supports Claudius's wish to have Hamlet cease mourning for his father and remain in Denmark rather than return to university, but does so in a considerate, kindly manner. "Let not thy mother lose her prayers," she says. Gertrude shows strength of will in supporting the king, but has Hamlet's welfare firmly in mind.

She shows concern for him when joining Claudius in welcoming Rosencrantz and Guildenstern to court. Gertrude tells them of the high regard Hamlet has for them, and promises a fitting reward if they are able to discover what has been troubling him. She urges them to visit Hamlet immediately.

When Claudius tells Gertrude that Polonius may have discovered the cause of Hamlet's madness, she is sceptical at first but is persuaded after Polonius puts his case. As he rambles on, however, the queen demands, "more matter, with less art" and interrupts when Polonius is critical of Hamlet's salutation in the letter to Ophelia. When she sees Hamlet approaching, Gertrude says, "sadly the poor wretch comes reading," an indication of distress and sympathy for him. The queen is assertive and very much on Hamlet's side.

As Rosencrantz and Guildenstern report their lack of success with Hamlet, Gertrude asks if he received them well and whether they were able to involve him in any diversions. Turning to Ophelia, who is about to encounter the prince in the nunnery scene, she says that she hopes the interview will prove that the loss of Hamlet's relationship with her is in fact the cause of his madness. The queen continues to advocate for her son.

Before the play-within-the-play begins, Hamlet declines his mother's invitation to sit by her, preferring to engage with Ophelia. When Hamlet asks her opinion of the play, Gertrude objects to the Player Queen's excessive promise never to remarry. Hamlet's response that she will keep her word is an indirect rebuke of Gertrude for marrying Claudius so quickly. Although Hamlet keeps his distance from her, Gertrude did ask him to join her and offers a candid opinion of the Player Queen's speech.

Before hiding behind the arras, Polonius instructs the queen to be direct with Hamlet, stressing that she has intervened on his behalf many times. When Gertrude challenges Hamlet for offending Claudius, he speaks of her offense against Old Hamlet. She reminds him of her status as queen and threatens to call for guards. As Hamlet tells her to sit and listen, her cries for help are echoed by Polonius, whom Hamlet stabs behind the arras. Gertrude calls the killing a "rash and bloody deed" and blames Hamlet for wagging his tongue rudely at her. She demands to know why she deserves his abuse. Gertrude is highly assertive in the face of his attack. She soon breaks down, however, becoming fully allied with her son. The queen's active support of Hamlet strengthens as she grows emotionally distant from Claudius.

iii

Hamlet's denunciation of women occurs prior to learning of Gertrude's seduction by Claudius and of the murder of Old Hamlet. He resents her failure to mourn his father's death sufficiently and her willingness to marry Claudius so quickly. Although these actions might indicate moral weakness on Gertrude's part, they hardly constitute grounds for accusing all women of frailty. The prince is over-reacting. As far as he knows, Gertrude's marriage could have been motivated by a need for personal security. She was the widow of a former monarch. The kingdom was unstable to the point where Young Fortinbras was demanding return of lands formerly belonging to Norway. The need for a quick marriage would have been strong. Hamlet was in unresolved mourning for his father and perhaps compensating by blaming his mother for disrespecting the memory of Old Hamlet.

It seems clear that Gertrude and Ophelia each displayed considerable strength of character throughout the play. Ophelia may have appeared weak for lapsing into insanity over the killing of her father and perhaps for failing to save herself from drowning. Gertrude might be regarded as weak for her adultery with Claudius and decision to marry him. However, the overall behaviour of Ophelia and Gertrude does not support Hamlet's assertion that frailty is the defining characteristic of womankind. Ophelia cared deeply for the prince and Gertrude always had his interests at heart. His mother's apparent disrespect to the memory of Old Hamlet may have intensified a negative attitude toward women already present in Hamlet. It may well have grown when Ophelia was forced to break off their relationship. Despite Gertrude's increasing support of Hamlet, all the prince can manage to say before he dies is, "Wretched queen, adieu!" This is short shrift for Gertrude and further evidence of misogyny in Hamlet.

To the Reader

I hope your experience with *Understanding Hamlet* has proved helpful and rewarding. Shakespeare is arguably the greatest dramatist in the Western tradition and *Hamlet* is his best-known and most studied work. As was mentioned in "Mighty Opposites", one of the reasons Prince Hamlet is such a memorable character is that many of us see something of ourselves mirrored in him. Perhaps it is his tendency to procrastinate in the face of daunting challenges or his helpless outrage at the enormity of the burden he is forced to assume. However that may be, I trust that readers of this book will have gained a clearer understanding of the challenge Hamlet struggles with and his inability or apparent unwillingness to cope with it.

R.R.

About the Author

Robert Renwick was born in Regina, Saskatchewan in 1938. The family moved to Hamilton, Ontario in 1950, where Renwick attended Delta Secondary School and McMaster University, graduating with a Bachelor of Arts degree in 1960. He also holds graduate degrees from the University of Toronto in English language and literature and in applied psychology.

Renwick's M.A. thesis explored tragic themes in Melville's *Moby-Dick*. In 1973-1974 he attended the graduate seminar in creative writing at the University of Windsor, directed by the American novelist Joyce Carol Oates. His article on higher education in Ontario, originally published in *The Globe and Mail*, was reprinted in *Contemporary Issues In Canadian Education* (1972). He has had a number of articles on education published over the years in teachers' magazines. *Understanding Hamlet* is his first published book.

Renwick taught English in Ontario secondary schools for 27 years, eight of which he served as department head. After retiring from teaching, he worked as a psychotherapist in the Regional Municipality of York in Ontario for 13 years. He resides there in Holland Landing.

You can find Robert online at:
facebook.com/UnderstandingHamlet
understandinghamlet.wordpress.com

To the Reader

CPSIA information can be obtained
at www.ICGtesting.com
Printed in the USA
LVHW110133190219
607988LV00001BA/35/P